Feisty & Fearless: Nice Girls CAN Be Leaders

Feisty & Fearless: Nice Girls CAN Be Leaders

PAULINE FIELD

Feisty & Fearless: Nice Girls CAN Be Leaders

This book is dedicated to my grandchildren
Katy, Ally, Kaitlyn, Cheyenne, Tatiana, Bella, Gabe, Avi, Maya

CONTENTS

Feisty & Fearless Challenges:
As I was writing this, it seemed that there were lessons I had learned that I wanted to make sure you had the chance to ponder and work on for yourself. Throughout the book are fourteen of these challenges and I hope you take the time to address them in your life.

ACKNOWLEDGEMENTS

This book owes a whole lot to a large group of people and without any one of them, it would not be complete. Let's start at the top: President Abraham Lincoln was a role model for me in so many ways. Thanks to AbrahamLincolnOnline.org for the timeline of failures he encountered on his way to becoming President of the United States. The United Nations is not only the peacemaker of the world; its website (www.un.org/en/) is a veritable library of information on the many topics in which it is involved. The website provided much valuable information.

Thanks also to the leaders I interviewed, who inspired me with their passion, commitment and willingness to share their stories: Jan Harrington, Leigh Adams, Maia Mossé, Ann Rector, Shelby Dietrich, Sharon Roszia, Kellie "Kacee" Clanton, Sarah Manor, Claudette Roche, Elisabeth Gortschacher, Pamela Kightlinger. The list goes on: Ria Severance for her friendship and belief in the bigger me, rather than my smaller, petty self. Barry Allen, my partner and soulmate, the person who listens to me when I need to be heard. Ellen Snortland, who taught me that I could write and told me consistently that my voice was needed. All the people in Ellen's writing group, who listened to pieces of the book as I wrote them. Kelly Hayes-Raitt, who urged me to continue with the book when I ran into dead ends.

These people proved invaluable in helping me develop my own leadership principles and style: Rafi Manoukian for his community-mindedness that started me on the path to the Women's Commission. The board members past and present, Leadership Circle members, Women of the World awardees, and volunteers of 50/50 Leadership who are committed to women's equal leadership. Reggie Odom for her skill and insightfulness in doing a hand analysis that brought me the clarity I needed to finish the book after it sat for many months untouched.

I can't forget Mary Ann Feeney, who turned me down when I asked her to edit the book and instead brought me together with the superb editor, Nona Strong, who helped me polish the book until it shone. Ilyanna Gutierrez for her incredible cover design and for enthusiastically jumping in to make that happen. Linda Lazar, who started me on the path to writing the book by telling me that the more she knew me, the more she was inspired to do because of what I had done as an *ordinary* person. If I could do some of the things I have, Linda said, she could envision that for herself. Alison Lewis for helping to get me out of my own way. Carolyn Howard-Johnson, who has been a great role model with her writing and her unstoppable marketing prowess.

I wouldn't have made it this far without Adrian Kirk Field, the light that brought me through dark times in my life. And last but not least, my mother, whose indomitable spirit is such a great role model for me.

FOREWORD

I have been passionate about women's rights since I was a teen. After reading Sisterhood is Powerful by Robin Morgan, I saw the *deficiencies* of being female not as personal flaws but basically acculturated lessons of what a *good* woman/girl was vs.what a *bad* woman/girl was. All *good* women were expected to be *nice* no matter what. I had been raised to be decorative, passive and inconsequential: all the qualities of nice. Nice is great but it only goes so far.

Feisty & Fearless: Nice Girls CAN Be Leaders takes a telescope to the constellation of issues that women face when learning to lead. Pauline Field, like so many girls and women, learned to get ahead by being nice, only to find that it was a double-edged sword or, let's say hammer. As Abraham Maslow said, "If the only tool you have is a hammer, everything starts to look like a nail." Ms. Field's *nice* hammer backfired when what she needed for some tasks was a saw, a screwdriver or even a jack-hammer when it came to standing up for what she believes. Courage often requires much more than nice.

This book provides stories and examples of regular women who have made a difference in their lives, families and communities. It also offers an opportunity for women who are serious about leadership to challenge themselves by doing the inner work necessary via the Feisty & Fearless Challenges that are within the chapters.

We need more women to step up and into their leadership potential! So please, read this book, do the work of the Feisty & Fearless Challenges, and join me in working for a more workable world for us all with no one and nothing left out. And you CAN keep your nice but when YOU choose it as a tool, not as your only default way of being.

Ellen Snortland, J.D., Author of Beauty Bites Beast and The Safety Godmothers; director and writer of the documentary "Beauty Bites Beast."

We have more laughter than the world has problems, more hugs than children have giggles and more wonder than we can imagine

Leigh Adams

1

NICE GIRLS CAN BE LEADERS

Despite the fact that I now am willing to give myself such titles as "feminist" and "leader," I have spent much of my life suppressing myself. I interpreted the social messages thrown at me through the filter of whether I was "nice": if I acted *nice*, all would be well. To this end, I eliminated the "f*** you's," other epithets and most anger, rage, fury, passion and yes, even love, from my communications. I am *nice*. This adjective has cost me a lot, but despite that, I have managed somehow to be a leader during several passages of my life. I have determined to keep *nice* to a minimum in this book. Discrimination is something I have experienced: as a woman, a Jew and an immigrant; for having red hair; too little money and too much; and for being fat. At the tender age of three I was told I was too "bossy." This book is the little red-haired, pushy, bossy, passionate kid inside getting out and saying "I *will* be heard." Thanks for listening.

When I read of our much-loved former U.S. President Abraham Lincoln's failures, defeats and heartbreaks, I started to have a glimmer that my life might also be worth something after all. So I did a comparison – oh yes, and nice girls don't brag or do things like compare themselves with a great person like President Lincoln. So much for nice; maybe I am off to a good start:

> Lost his job in 1832
> Defeated for the Legislature in 1832
> Failed in business in 1833
> Elected to Legislature in 1834
> Suffered death of sweetheart in 1835
> Had nervous breakdown in 1836
> Defeated for Speaker in 1838
> Defeated for nomination to Congress in 1843
> Elected to Congress in 1846
> Lost renomination in 1848
> Rejected for Land Office in 1849
> Defeated for the Senate in 1854
> Defeated for nomination for Vice President in 1856
> Again defeated for the Senate in 1858
> But... in 1860,
> Abraham Lincoln was elected President of the United States of America

Here's a sampling of my path, by age:

> 16 – Graduated from high school (barely)
> 17 – Dropped out of college after one year
> 18 – Laid off from my first job
> 19 – Fired from my second job
> 20 – Left the next job to move to the United States
> 21–25 – Fired from each of several other secretarial jobs
> 29 – Pregnant, homeless and living in a tent
> 29 – Gave birth to son, Adrian Kirk Field

29 – Lost my father, Lionel Isadore Shenker, who died two weeks later

30 – Miscarried second child

32 – Became top salesperson within three months at my first sales job

32 – Fired nine months later for poor performance

33 – Fired from next sales job for poor performance

34 – Found the field of consulting

34 – Landed project with Fortune 100 company; halfway through, the company decided to close down the department

34–38 – Built a thriving consulting practice

35 – Made first appearances on television and radio

36 – Raised most money ever in annual appeal for local synagogue

37 – Chaired most successful fundraiser at annual gala

38 – Acquired another consulting firm and a partner

39 – Discovered husband was jealous of partner

43 – Sold the consulting firm to my partner

43 – Divorced husband

43 – Joined another consulting firm

43 – Was quickly promoted

44 – Almost fired six months later

46–48 – Ran three marathons

48 – Started second consulting firm

49 – Found soulmate and business partner rolled into one

51 – Grew consulting firm so fast that we were invited to be included in *Inc.* magazine's list of fastest growing consulting firms

54 – Created a Women's Commission as part of the Glendale, California city government

55 – Founded non-profit organization, 50/50 Leadership, to promote women's equal leadership

55 – Was invited onto board of local chapter of United Nations Association

55–56 – Served as a commissioner on the Glendale Women's Commission

57 – Ran for election to Glendale City Council. Most votes per dollars spent. Lost election

59 – Invited onto board of local Girl Scouts Council

60 – Invited to become a U.S. Ambassador for World Leadership Day

61 – Left consulting. Took first job outside of consulting in twenty-seven years

62 – Became grandma to Tatiana Marie. Job#1

65 – Appointed to the board of the national women's group at work

66 – Received MVP award at work

Whew!

Neither of these lists sounds like a recipe for leadership in my mind. So as I was considering this book, several questions came up. Questions like, how old do you have to be to be a leader? Why are there more men leaders? Does having a title make you a leader? Why is the world such a mess if we know what leadership is about? Do men make better leaders? Do women? Do you have to be born a leader?

I watched playgrounds and saw leaders aged 3, 4 and 7. I met with a woman of 87 who is leading the way in helping others younger than she move forward in their lives. With these and the many other examples of leaders between those ages, I concluded that age has nothing much to do with leadership.

Thousands of years ago in Egypt, women ruled. There are a few matriarchies in the world, but today, men vastly outnumber women as leaders in the highest positions. Men make more of the rules regarding women than women do. Many women are just fine with that. Ellen Johnson Sirleaf has been transforming Liberia since she was elected as the country's president. Angela Merkel, as prime minister of Germany, has been guiding one of the world's richest nations for several years. John F. Kennedy, former president of the United States, brought pride and prosperity to our country. Oprah Winfrey defied her family's poverty mindset to become a leader in the entertainment industry. Nelson Mandela ended apartheid in South Africa. From this handful of examples it seems clear that even at the top, in positions where often millions of lives are at stake, women and men can be equally great leaders.

Consider if there were ninety-five women heads of state; that is very close to half the member countries of the United Nations. Would women leaders be seen in a different light? Would the world be more peaceful? Would we be kinder to the environment? What if 250 CEOs of the Fortune 500 companies in the U.S. were women, half the U.S. senators and members of the House of Representatives were women, twenty-five state governors were women? Might there be different thinking about gender as a factor in leadership with that kind of balance? I suspect so.

As you read this book, I hope you see yourself in some of the stories and gain strength from knowing that as I have risen above many obstacles, so can you. There are a few challenges that I have set for you, should you want to engage. You will see them as **Feisty & Fearless Challenges**. Let's continue now, as I recount my journey; then we'll visit the stories of a few leaders I have met along the way.

■ ■ ■

The leaders who are featured in the book are a varied group of women and a few men, and so that you can know a little about them, here is a brief profile of each.

Leigh Adams is a multitalented artist who brings art to children and public places and is also helping bring desert landscaping back to the Los Angeles area.

Adora Svitak is an activist and internationally published author. Teaching since before she was a teenager, she knows that kids are leaders too.

Ria Severance is a licensed therapist, an executive coach, divorce options specialist, parenting counselor and the mother of two successful children.

Maia Mossé is a medical student at Stanford University, runs an award-winning nonprofit organization, went to Honduras on a Fulbright Scholarship, and is one of Ria Severance's children.

Kacee sings on Broadway, in Los Angeles, and around the world.

Elisabeth Gortschacher is a certified life coach in Australia and works with leaders around the world. Elisabeth founded World Leadership Day.

Adel Luzuriaga is a real estate agent and community activist, and manages the many properties she owns.

Sarah Manor created her life from scratch and now is the assistant director of the school her children attend.

Jan Harrington started a construction company at a time when it was almost unknown for a woman to be involved in that industry.

Ann Rector is in charge of the healthy children programs at the Pasadena Unified School District.

Claudette Roche is a dialect coach, removing and adding accents not only to actors but also to executives.

Kristi Toia is the CEO of her family's business, Glendale Builders Supply.

Ellen Snortland has a law degree and is a feminist, performer, activist, self-defense trainer, published author and filmmaker.

Pamela Kightlinger takes the role of leader when presented with opportunities to contribute in areas about which she is passionate.

Sharon Kaplan Roszia is a world-renowned expert on child adoption, has published twelve books and has been quoted countless times by the media.

Dr. Shelby Dietrich is a retired physician and the proud mother of Ann Rector.

Linda Lazar, licensed therapist and web developer, and CEO of IrishLemons.com. Linda created and maintains all my websites, including 50/50 Leadership.org, PaulineField.com, and Coach4Women.com.

Tiffany Persons is a commercial casting director and founded the nonprofit Shine On Sierra Leone.

Reggie Odom has been an athletic coach, national sports official and is now a life coach and trainer.

Rafi Manoukian is a CPA, was a Glendale City Council member and mayor, and is now City Treasurer of the City of Glendale, California.

Dan Price is CEO of Gravity Payments, Inc. and has happy employees.

Phlunté Riddle is a retired police officer, completed her PhD, is a business consultant and running for election to the California State Senate.

2

FIRED TO FIRED UP – TURNING FAILURES INTO STEPPING STONES

Seventeen, finished with a year of community college in London, England, I was clueless as a butterfly as I flitted from job to job. Once unshackled from the chains of school, I felt free. Now in the adult world with a job, money in my pocket, and the independence to come and go as I wished, I felt very much alive.

I knew I wanted to have fun, and that meant boys, clothes, dancing, music, travel, and friends mixed in a bottomless cocktail of life.

Responsibility? Not me. I had enough of that from my somewhat Victorian and rigid upbringing. I wanted none of it. Smart enough to know what would get me a job, I found my first one out of college with a travel agency. I pictured myself jetting around the world being wined and dined by princes and movie stars. Soon enough I discovered that coming into work each day, having to pay attention, learn office politics – who was gossiping about whom – was anything but glamorous.

Of course I managed to add some fun to work too. Kenye worked in a curtained off area behind where I sat, and he was always smiling, shining a brilliantly white smile that lit up his dark brown face and made his eyes sparkle. I enjoyed our friendship but had no idea that he was thinking of something more than an office friendship, so of course I was surprised when he asked me out on a date. Here came my first realization of my own inauthenticity. While I thought I was a liberal thinker, I was plunged into having to decide between having fun on a date with him and suffering the consequences of my parents' views. I took the low road and went for the easier playmates that I could get past mom and dad.

Other than a few such hiccups, though, through my twenties I remained adamantly rebellious, defiant, and an independent spirit that answered to no one. Clearly I could not have been termed a responsible adult at that time, but as I had not found a career, my job was just a job. It was no surprise then that each year, from my first job in the travel agency and thereafter, I was fired. Was I bothered? The first time, yes, I was crushed. I thought I would never find another job, that I was a loser and would have to live with my parents forever. What happened, however, was that I kept getting better jobs with more pay and bigger titles. So with no consequences for my irresponsibility, I learned mostly arrogance. I interviewed my potential bosses rather than feeling that I was going hat in hand looking for each job. With no incentive to change my ways, I didn't.

I started each job with enthusiasm; I was willing to show just how good a job I could do. But before long I settled in, laid back and indulged in constant chattering – to my coworkers and on the phone, and putting off doing any work each day as long as I could.

If you hear some pride in all this, you're hearing it right. I had no shame. In my head, it was their problem, their loss, and I was more than ready each time to move on. How could I be so arrogantly insensitive? I justified it easily with the story that it was the kind of work my parents thought I should be doing. I'd wanted to be a beautician, so this was just another ridiculously childish way of getting back at my parents.

I really had no idea what kind of work I wanted to do. Truth be told, I just wanted to play. Although I would have denied it at the time, being somewhat of a feminist, albeit a closet one, I wanted what was expected of me: to settle down and marry a nice man who would take care of me, and I would be a housewife with a nice big house, in the right area of course, a white picket fence and two lovely children.

At the age of twenty, off I went to New York (more about that later). It meant I was even further away from my parents and responsibility, and being in a new city, I could be and do what I wanted as no one knew me. If I failed, I could always run home to London.

New York seemed like London on steroids. I loved the life of London, and New York was bigger and faster. With my British accent and my mini-skirts, I suddenly was more popular than I had ever been, with as many dates as I wanted, making more money than I had in London, even new girlfriends. I was in heaven.

Eddie, who became husband number one, came on the scene fairly quickly and between us we had lots of friends, most of whom were in college. That seemed challenging in a fun way, so I decided to join in and enrolled at Hunter College.

Despite a constant stream of self-doubts, fears, and poor-me's, I also had a lot of confidence. My mother had reminded me that as a teenager, I said I could talk to strangers because I knew they were just as afraid of me, so I might as well give them a smile and talk to them.

As I was fired from each job, I didn't make up a story about how bad I was, how much of a loser I was, although those thoughts crossed my mind. Instead I chose the other story playing in my head, the one that said I could have any job I wanted – that being fired was a good thing.

One summer in New York I had been fired from a job and decided to take the summer off: three months of play, yummy. This worked out well because Eddie and I lived simply in New York. We enjoyed our friends and the free or cheap entertainment available in Greenwich Village, Central Park, museums, coffee houses, and more. Life was luscious, especially when you broke the rules.

Although I was fired a lot, I was fired up a lot too: my first semester of college I was fired up at the thought of being there. Me, at university, the kid who hated school and went to one year of college in London only because my parents dragged me. The girl who only wanted to play was finally doing homework and writing papers and reading books; listening to music by dead composers that I had previously only scoffed at; and loving sociology, anthropology and statistical methodology. I had conversations about things other than boys, clothes and gossip; subjects like politics, philosophy and how to end world hunger were now what I talked about. I wanted to be part of the solution to the problems in the world; I wanted to make a difference.

A few years later, with Gary, husband number two, I discovered I was pregnant. I was fired up and determined to give my baby a great start in life. I went to La Leche League to learn about breastfeeding. I learned what to eat and drink, and what not to, so that the fetus could grow to its fullest potential. I also knew I needed to work out how I could be there for the first couple of years of my baby's life.

The fire in me didn't always burn brightly. Sometimes it seemed to go out, leaving hardly a glimmering ember. Like when I lived in a tent for several months during my pregnancy, blaming my husband who couldn't or wouldn't get a job. The fire never got so low again once my son, Adrian, was born. Always my beacon in life's storms, he has been the light that gives meaning to my life whenever I have thought there was none.

Fast-forward to the years after Adrian left home and I met the love of my life, Barry. I was fired up about one thing after another in those years. Finding my true mate at the age of 49 fired me up.

Starting a business with him as my partner fired me up. I wanted to start another management consulting firm, and as Barry and I discussed what I had seen as the good, the bad and the ugly of other firms, ideas flew until we came up with what was then an innovative business model, which was immediately picked up by the *Los Angeles Times*. That brought us more business and consultants to join our ranks. Growing the firm as quickly as we did was heady stuff, and I loved it. We were able to travel not just for business, but for pleasure also. There seemed to be no stopping us. I tingled with aliveness as I romped through it all. Life was very good.

In the middle of all this heat, along came another fire the likes of which I had not experienced since I had first discovered consulting: I found my inner feminist. This had been a pilot light in my twenties and until this time, I had rebuffed any attempt to turn up the gas. Here it was now, in full flame.

I threw myself into the cause of women's equal leadership, and it burns in me still.

After leading the charge to create a women's commission in the City of Glendale, the fire needed more fuel and I founded 50/50 Leadership, a nonprofit to transform the culture to allow women to be chosen as leaders on an equal basis with men. My vision was that 50 percent of leaders should be women. With that vision and the sorry state of unequal leadership, I knew I had something to work on for a long time. And I knew I had to take this on as a long-term commitment.

For seven years 50/50 Leadership partnered with the United Nations Association of Pasadena to honor local women who had answered the call of service in other countries. Tiffany Persons, founder of Shine on Sierra Leone and one of our first honorees, is a commercial casting director in the entertainment world. Tiffany was on location in Sierra Leone to produce a documentary and had lived in a diamond mining community for three months when she encountered the eager faces of children in a classroom with no roof. These children wanted to learn, but some days the torrential rain made the task almost impossible. She also learned that some of the children ate only every few days, making it hard for them to learn.

Rather than just being sad for these children, Tiffany took it upon herself to do something about it, raising money to put a roof on the schoolhouse, providing food for the children, and founding Shine on Sierra Leone, which today is a nonprofit whose mission is to create sustainable programs to promote thriving, self-sufficient communities. With this opportunity Tiffany had a whole new purpose to her life, as well as being a great role model for her daughter.

Not all leaders fall into leadership; some leaders know they want to lead and set about doing it. Either way, there is leadership that the world needs, and some that we don't. For the sake of clarity, I will use "leader" when speaking of the first, "mercenary" when referring to the latter.

I was not always ready to step up; sometimes I was quite reluctant, which brings me to my next story.

3

RELUCTANT LEADER –FROM BOSSY TO BOSS

Why *reluctant*? Because at the tender age of three, I was told I was too *bossy*, and promptly made up my mind that I should just fall in line rather than trying to take the lead.

Did this stop me? Yes and no. As you will see throughout the book, I have taken leadership roles on many different occasions but have favored supporting roles, such as vice president, rather than top dog. Why not president or CEO? Because the three-year-old in me was convinced that being boss equaled being *bossy*, and that was not a good thing. Even when I was Chair of the Board of my own company, I agreed to be Chief Operations Officer (COO), not Chief Executive Officer (CEO). Old decisions die hard.

As I have accomplished things in life (and have been acknowledged for many of them), I nevertheless consider myself just a regular person striving to do what I can to make this world a better place for my family, my community and me. I have made many mistakes, some quite large, and sometimes it has taken me a while to overcome the circumstances of my life.

But I now know that in my small corner of the world, I have made (and continue to make) a difference for people, and I am writing this book to help you see that even if you do not think of yourself as a leader, you can gain confidence from my account of my own experience: how ordinary I am, how many mistakes I have made. Against this backdrop, you may discover how you, too, can be a leader and make a difference.

After attending a workshop by Reggie Odom on Stepping Into Your Greatness, I was able to look back and see that at different times in my life, an opportunity presented itself and I took it on.

When I was nineteen I had a friend in London who said she was going to the American embassy to start the process of getting a green card so she could emigrate to New York, where her mother was living. She reminded me that I had told her I would go back to the Big Apple someday, and she asked if I wanted to come with her to the embassy and go through the process on my own behalf. I did, and a year later I came back to New York and have lived in the United States ever since.

I had never liked my work and had always known that I wanted to do something else. Frances, a friend I had made in New York during my wild-and-crazy days, had been working in sales at IBM and said she thought I would be great at sales. I couldn't imagine doing that, but I went for it. I followed Frances' direction, picking a few companies that I thought I might be interested in working for. One lunchtime I took my résumé over to one company's offices. While I was speaking to the receptionist, asking that my résumé be given to the sales manager, he walked by, heard what I was saying, invited me into his office and interviewed me on the spot. He hired me a few days later, and within months I was the top salesperson.

After I had been through several sales positions, I knew it was time to move on again to something different. I went to workshops and conferences, networked, and did informational interviews; but nothing seemed right until my husband Duane (spouse number three) suggested I do consulting. I didn't have much of an idea what a consultant did or what it took to be a consultant, but I decided to find out.

Once I started I felt like I had come home. I was using the talents I had been given and the skills and education I had gained.

Elisabeth Gortschacher, Founder of World Leadership Day describes a leader as one whose "actions, choices and words align with your soul's purpose. It is not about how many people follow your vision. It is about how fully aligned you are in expressing your soul's purpose in the world." I had found the purpose for my life for the next twenty-seven years.

Finding our purpose is one of the great quests of life, and sometimes when we are presented a path, we decline it. Just today I heard of a woman who regrets that when she was offered a place at university with a full scholarship, she turned it down because she was scared. Of all the people I interviewed, and often in my own journey, I have been frightened by all the "what if's": What if I fail? What if I am no good at it? What if no one likes me? What if …?

My hope is that the stories in this book will help you make the choices to be the leader in your family, at work or in your community.

Feisty & Fearless Challenge #1:

Are there any opportunities you have let go by? If so, write them down. Then, if you have feelings of regret, write about those too. Include the what if's (what if I had done this or that, what if I had said yes instead of no, etc.). The act of writing it all down will help you with the next step, which is to forgive yourself. That will free you up to move on and take on the next opportunity that comes your way.

4

PROBLEMS WITH LEADERSHIP TODAY: DOES IT HAVE TO BE JUST ABOUT PROFIT?

A couple of years ago I proposed that people who achieved great financial success would serve the world well if they took their talents and turned them toward solving the ills of the world. After all, if leadership is strictly for the purpose of profit, is that really leadership or just accomplishing a set of goals? For billionaires to become so successful they clearly have something that the rest of us do not, and leadership is one of their traits. Unfortunately, compassion and caring and bringing opportunity to all has not often been the top of their list of interests. It was with delight, then, that I read of Bill Gates' and Warren Buffett's endeavors to persuade billionaires to give away at least half of their money.

Giving away that much money is not just about writing a check. The Bill & Melinda Gates Foundation for instance, looks very carefully at the projects it funds, and is careful to choose projects that fit its mission and values, and that stand a good chance of having a considerable impact in the community. Also, Bill and his wife Melinda are active in many of these projects, adding their own leadership skills to ensure success.

When considering what it takes to be a leader interested in the common good rather than just in one's own power, it is useful to look at the criteria that we so often use to determine whether a person is ready for and capable of such leadership. While formal education is useful, it is not the only determinant for success — in leadership or anything else. Does that mean that people with PhDs, MBAs and other degrees cannot be great leaders? Of course not. It just points out that we have to be a little more judicious in our choice of criteria when selecting leaders. Having dropped out of graduate school myself, I have become more aware of successful dropouts than of some of my more educated friends.

Part of the problem with leadership today is that the whole idea of leadership has been created by men, for men. Despite women leaders being prominently acknowledged in the media, women's voices as a whole have been heard too infrequently to have much input into what makes a leader. What we need is a richer, more complete definition of leadership that includes women and what we bring to the equation. Looking at the general discourse on leadership, we need to notice what is missing and consider what a true transformation in the culture of leadership would look like. A more purposeful narrative, that is more than just about reaching a goal or having hordes of people following, is essential.

In an article in *Time* magazine, Rana Foroohar equates the rise of the MBA with the fall of American industry. She notes that the people who were interested in innovation, technology, and listening to the customer were shooed into the background to make way for the financial people. Only profit, and how much, was of interest. Short-term money goals outweighed long-term interests of the company, the economy, and the environment.

This balance-sheet-driven management style was almost the demise of Apple, for instance, when Steve Jobs, a college dropout, first left the company. It wasn't until he came back that innovation returned and the company became the powerhouse it is today.

Richard Branson, founder of the Virgin companies, of which Virgin Airways, Virgin Music, and Virgin America are just a few of the more prominent, is a college dropout. Yet his companies have been trailblazers, have high customer ratings, *and* make lots of money.

Barbara Lynch was not burdened with an MBA, yet she built a restaurant group in Boston, Massachusetts worth several million dollars.

Christine Comaford-Lynch is an author and the founder of Artemis Ventures, a venture capital firm, and Mighty Ventures. She dropped out of high school, University of California at San Diego and UCLA.

There were people who would not hire me as a management consultant because I did not have an MBA, yet on more than one occasion, I was hired to come in after the MBAs had been there, in order to clean up the messes they had made.

Where is the end to this blindness that keeps the corporate world focused on this quarter's earnings? It is important that we strive for transformation of what we expect from our leaders, what effective leadership really is.

While our blindness might just cause frustration in dealing with companies whose products and services are decidedly customer-unfriendly, it is particularly unsettling when we consider the food industry. Some say we are eating animals loaded with antibiotics, which are now being seen as a threat to our health as new bacterial strains grow stronger and more resistant, sometimes ahead of the science to counteract them. Research is showing more and more negative effects of the quantities of sugar we are eating. Can we really call the people heading these companies *leaders*? I would call them *mercenaries*. Their chief aim is making money and increasing their power, with no concern for the negative effects of their actions on their companies, employees, customers, and the world around them. Yet these people still manage to sleep at night and find ways to justify the damage they are wreaking, all in the name of profit and power.

Desperate is the need for leaders who look at the bigger picture, who are willing to say "no" to destructive answers to the problems facing us. As long as leaders are ego-focused, when they will not find the time or take the risk of finding the high road, we will continue to imperil life as we know it. To feed, clothe, transport, educate, entertain, and keep healthy a growing population, we need courageous leaders willing to speak truth to power. We need leaders who are willing to put their jobs on the line if necessary for the sake of what they know is right.

Mercenaries are too comfortable in their well-heeled lives, greedy to hang on to their luxurious lifestyles, unwilling to do anything that will lessen the growth of their empires, much less put their positions in jeopardy.

Leadership is not static. Even the best leaders can lose their way. Iceland experienced years of great leadership that resulted in an almost idyllic life for its residents. Then the country's leaders lost focus and passed laws that did not have all Icelandic people in mind and that ultimately led to financial devastation, high unemployment and huge debt.

Law enforcement in this country has veered away from its mission *to protect and serve*. Minorities, particularly young men, are targeted by police officers simply because they are a minority. Too often they suffer from unreasonable, uncalled for violence against them. Research shows that women police officers are more effective than male officers at defusing situations without the use of excessive force, yet few women make it to the leadership ranks, where they could help spread a culture that is about keeping the peace rather than creating conflict.

There is no silver bullet, no single answer about how to transform leadership, but we must strive to develop leaders who have a conscience and who are willing to ask the tough questions.

It is up to each one of us to step up, speak up, and be an example of leadership that works for all of us, not just some of us.

The scientist Margaret Mead said it very eloquently:

Never doubt that a small group of thoughtful, committed citizens can change the world; indeed, it's the only thing that ever has.

5

LEADER OR MERCENARY: WHICH WILL YOU BE?

Writing a book on leadership seemed a little bizarre to me given one of the views I have of myself. But then again, maybe it is not so bizarre. When I was busy beating myself up over my third divorce, about how I was a loser who couldn't pick or keep a husband, I met Kelly Hayes-Raitt, who spoke of the courage her mother had in marrying for the sixth time.

Courage

I rarely think of myself as courageous. I am, however, and so are you. We all are. We all face doubts and feelings of insufficiency. Some days just getting up in the morning takes courage.

This book is about going to work when you just don't think you can get out of bed. It's about raising your hand when there's a call for volunteers and no one else is stepping up. It's about saying, "Here I am." We are all leaders. This is about polishing ourselves up, celebrating our successes *and* our failures. As you saw at the beginning of the book, I have had failures, and it took me a long time to see them as the stepping stones that kept me moving forward.

As someone once said to me, when you fall flat on your face, at least it is forward motion.

Through interviews, Internet research, and paying attention to examples of leadership that I encountered, it became clear that although there are a few traits common to mercenaries and leaders, such as the ability to get things done or make things happen, there are many others that are only on the leader side of the chart.

Responsibility

Let's start with *responsibility*. What does this word really mean? When interviewing leaders for this book, it became apparent that responsibility is about being willing to take on our individual lives rather than to be victims of fate, circumstances, birth, and so on. As you read their stories, you will see that each of the leaders we are looking at did just that. We all have times in our lives when we are faced with the opportunity to rise above what life is giving us, or resign ourselves to being victims of it, and sometimes we just cannot seem to muster the strength, or the will, or both.

As I have mentioned, I had no interest in being responsible; I was waiting for my White Knight to come along and make everything wonderful. Being responsible for ourselves does not preclude us from reaching out for help and support from others. It does mean finding the strength that lives within us to take life on, to make the choice for the life and circumstances we really would rather have.

Accountability

Sister to responsibility is accountability. While responsibility is an internal choice about being proactive in our life rather than being resigned to whatever life throws our way, accountability is how we show up for others. Children need to know they can count on their parent(s) for the basics of life: food, shelter, love, and caring. We count on friends, coworkers, religious and political leaders, and when they do not come through, it can be distressing at best. We can step up to the plate and be accountable, or when we don't make good on our commitments, our promises and our responsibilities, we disappoint people, let them down, and become a barrier to progress. That is not to say we will never drop the ball; we do. It is how we clean up the mess that makes us leaders, or does not.

When we place blame on someone else or on circumstances, we let people down; if we just shrug our shoulders as if we have nothing to do with it, or as if it is not important that we didn't get the information for the report or pick our child up from school when school finishes, in those cases we are not being leaders.

Integrity

Following closely comes *integrity*. One of the definitions of integrity is *the state of being whole*. When we break the shell of an egg, we shatter its integrity. Applied to leadership, it is easy to see that when we say we will do something and when we actually do what we say we will do, in the time we said we would do it, we have closed the loop; we have kept our integrity. Our word, what we say, is what people can use to know us: it is what determines whether people will respect us, trust us ... or not. Politics is an easy place to observe what happens when integrity is lost. How often are we disappointed, frustrated, even angry at the unkept campaign promises once a politician is elected? At work, how much harder is your job because of people who fail to file a report on time or get you the information they said they would?

Phlunté Riddle, my co-chair for two years in putting on the Women of the World Awards, is a person of integrity, and what a difference that made. When Phlunté said she would take something on, I was able to move onto something else because I knew she was as good as her word – that what she said she would do, I could count on being done.

Risk-Taking

Most people we think of as leaders do things that we might not think ourselves capable of, but maybe they are just willing to take a risk. Many studies have shown that women tend to be more risk-averse than men, wanting to have all our ducks in a row before we jump in on a project or take on a new job. As women, we want to be at least 80 percent certain that we know what we are doing, whereas men need only be inspired by the challenge, thinking that they can figure it out as they go along. With this thinking, women lose out on opportunities that can mean the loss of hundreds of thousands of dollars over a career lifetime, and perhaps more important, the satisfaction of accomplishing at a level we were not sure was possible for us.

As with any generalization, there are always exceptions. When her high school class was asked for a volunteer to design and make a float for a parade, Leigh Adams raised her hand. She had no idea how to make a float, but she raised her hand anyway. She took a risk.

When we are sure of ourselves and our purpose, it is easier to take a risk. The work we do to understand our strengths and our mission in life makes taking on the mantle of leadership easier. We can raise our hand, open our mouths and step into the opportunity, not even thinking of the risk.

Openness

Leaders are open with everyone on their team, while mercenaries, afraid that someone else will beat them to the top or take away their power, are not. Openness is a way to empower your team because when you let them in on the setbacks and the challenges as well as the successes, they can see you are not perfect, so it gives them room to try and fail. How much easier for children to see their value and confidence in their abilities when they see a parent fail and then move on to the next step.

Several of the leaders highlighted in this book mentioned directly or indirectly the need to be open, whether it is to directly empower students as when Leigh Adams led her students in planning and going on a camping trip, Jan Harrington being forthright with her employees about what needs to be done and how her business is doing, Sarah Manor talking openly to her children about her divorce, or Kacee getting the cast together when there is a problem to talk it through.

A high percentage of the workforce in this country is disengaged, so just think how much more productive we all would be if our managers were more open with us. This of course presumes that managers are leaders, but one does not necessarily follow the other. A leader has a vision; a manager follows the rules. Do an Internet search on *Leadership Development* and you will find pages of entries for classes being offered at universities, corporations and consulting or training firms across the country, so the need is recognized. Unfortunately there are hundreds of thousands of managers who are not given the opportunity to be trained as leaders and who do not take it upon themselves to become leaders.

Although the culture of an organization is mostly determined by the person at the helm, much can be done at any level. A leader can emerge from anywhere; all it takes is the willingness to put your head up, look around, and speak up. If you are a manager, are you empowering your direct reports to be creative and innovative, or merely to do what they're told? Are you reaching out above you and to others in your organization with ideas that could help them and the whole unit or department or division or company?

A leader looks at the rules and determines which ones need to be followed, and which need reworking. Change comes only when someone is willing to take a risk. Are you ready?

When we speak we are afraid our words will not be heard or welcomed. But when we are silent, we are still afraid. So it is better to speak.

Audre Lorde

Feisty & Fearless Challenge #2:
What ideas do you have for doing things differently at work? If you have research to back up your ideas, that's great. Suggestions for how to implement your ideas, even better. Take the risk, speak up and make your voice heard.

Listening

Listening seems so simple; after all, it is something we do all day long. It turns out that most of us are not too good at it. Jan Harrington says, "As a leader I have to listen and hear effectively – and I don't mean I think of my next answer to what they're saying. I mean I really click in and listen to what they're saying. Maybe they have something to impart to me I haven't seen before." How often have you experienced your supervisor or manager really hearing what you have to say? If you are in sales, are you really listening to your customer or potential customer, or are you just seeing how you can make them buy what you are selling?

This year I attended two *speed networking* events: one where almost everyone was a salesperson, the other where most of the people were business owners. The difference was striking. I knew that at the first event the only thing they were listening for was the title I carried and whether I was the decision-maker for buying their category of products or services. If it was established that I couldn't help them sell something, I could have recited the phone book for all they listened to me.

At the second event, where most participants were business owners, it was a very different story. These people wanted to build a relationship. They wanted to know about me, what I did, my interests, and so on. They knew that even if I was not in the market for what they were selling, I might know someone who might want to buy.

The salespeople who tuned me out lost any opportunity for referrals from me. They forgot that sales is about relationship building.

Listening is important in all parts of our lives, not just at work. Have you been in conversation with someone who won't let you get a word in? Some weeks it seems like all the people I meet or have to work with have closed their ears and opened their mouths. Talk, talk, talk, endlessly. I admit, I tune them out after a while.

Given my experience that people are not so good at listening, I know people don't always hear me. Here's an example: Recently at a restaurant Barry ordered a steak "very, very rare." He really likes his steak close to raw. I wondered if the waiter had understood him though, because he seemed very off-handed as he took our orders. Sure enough, when our food came, Barry's steak was very, very well done. Obviously the waiter was expecting to hear *very well done*, and so that's what he passed on to the kitchen.

If you are asking someone to do something, it is often a good idea to have them repeat back to you what you are asking; that way you can confirm you are both on the same page, making it more probable you will get what you asked. Be aware of when you are really heard, and when you are not.

Knowing how to listen is not as easy as you might think, but when you encounter someone who really listens, you know it. You are heard, and it is a lovely feeling because we know we have connected with someone. As a management consultant and business coach my job was to listen, and I am very aware of how we all love to talk, but how rare it is for someone to listen. Last year someone was recommended to me as a potential board member for 50/50 Leadership, and I set up a meeting to have coffee with her. I left that meeting feeling very glad of the opportunity to meet her and to have her on the board, because she listened. There was dialogue instead of monologue. It was so refreshing.

Feisty & Fearless Challenge #3:
Maybe there is a reason we have two ears and only one mouth. For the next week, notice your conversations throughout the day – who

is doing the talking, who is listening. Mentally grade you and the other person(s) on how you and they did on the listening and hearing scale. Did you really listen and did they really stop talking and listen attentively? When did you and they never listen so it was clearly a monologue, even a short one?

You will no doubt learn something about how you and those around you communicate. With that knowledge, I challenge you to become a better listener and see how everyone around you changes.

Engagement

I have referred to this previously, but what does *engagement* really mean? A simple analogy is to think of the times when you are driving and you suddenly wonder how you got *here* when you were just *there* a second ago. Well, now think about times during the day or week when you are not present to your life. Being engaged in life, at work or at school, in the project at hand, is really about being *present*. Recent studies have shown that 70 percent of workers are not really engaged on a daily basis. That results in billions of dollars of lost productivity, creativity and innovation because people are not valued, engaged or empowered. Mercenaries see everything through the lens of their money, power, and prestige; they do not see that empowering others would ultimately benefit them too. Many managers are not present; they are mindlessly passing on the work that has been passed down to them. They are not thinking about the bigger picture, just about getting through the day without too many hassles.

How do you get more engaged? One place to start is attitude. If you don't enjoy where you are working or the job you are doing, you have choices. Whether or not you have the choice to change jobs, you do have the choice of what you bring to it.

When I left consulting I took a job that felt like I had sat at the top of a big slide and landed at the bottom. Instead of working with executives of major corporations, I was now an hourly worker, punching a clock, and having to follow the rules that someone else had made. If I had a problem I had to go to my supervisor, not to the CEO. I wish I could say that I changed my attitude towards my new job easily and effortlessly, but that was not the case. Many an afternoon I came home frustrated, angry, and wondering if I was totally nuts to have taken this job in the first place, and to be staying in it. I stuck with it though, and little by little I chipped away at my attitude and became grateful for my job, eager to do excellent work, and built good relationships along the way. As I write this book, I still have that job, enjoy it and am well-compensated for the work I do.

Feisty & Fearless Challenge #4:
Want to improve your job? Start by writing down everything you have to say about it – the good, the bad and the ugly. Put it all down; don't worry, no one else ever has to see this, so you can be brutally truthful. It feels good to acknowledge all that hurt, rage, sadness, regret and whatever other feelings are there.

Now write down why you like the job and what you are grateful for about it. If you are like me, this takes a little longer. Once when I took this challenge myself, I found that when I was ready to write all the bad, I didn't want to even consider that there was *anything* good about the job for which I could be grateful. It turned out to be a longer list than I had expected, and yours maybe also. You may want to keep this list handy so you can add to it over the next few days as you realize things you appreciate.

The next step is to look at your first writing and see what you can do about any of it. Is there a relationship that you can improve on with a coworker? Can you make the choice to take something or someone on and transform the situation? This is perhaps the hardest step because it involves looking internally and being honest about your part in the situation. In every one of the situations you have not been happy about, you have been involved. So take a look at what you can do differently.

One thing that has worked for me is to pick someone I really can't stand and write about why I am grateful for them. This might sound counterintuitive, but try it; something will come to mind. One thing I often try with people I don't like is to look at the stress *they* are under and how grateful I am for the work they are doing, despite the pressure. Do they work at home or at other offsite places some days? Perhaps that is something to be grateful for, as it gives you a little breathing room to get your work done.

When you do this exercise you will get some relief, and whether you stay in the job or move on, you will be better able to negotiate your way through problems and be a better colleague to all.

Empowerment

Empowerment is a sometimes overused word, but it's one that speaks volumes. There are so many ways, large and small, in which we can *empower* another, a group of people, and ourselves. It is about reaching in and pulling out the bigger part of each person. We all have our small, petty thoughts, ideas, habits, and attitudes, but we all can rise to the occasion to be bigger than that. This might simply be speaking to a young girl in a way that lets her know the difference she makes as part of the household when she sets the dinner table and cleans her room; or when you set up a team to complete a project and let the team members know you value their input and creativity.

President Kennedy empowered the whole aerospace industry by setting the goal to put a man (not a woman, but let's not go there) on the moon and bring him back safely to earth, all within a decade. The aerospace community thought it could not be done, that science was not far enough along. But President Kennedy's vision, his stand for that possibility, brought those scientists and engineers up several notches, to a point at which they overcame their doubts and created the solutions to make it happen.

Mistakes and failures are everyday occurrences, but if you try to be perfect and hold everyone on your team to a similar standard, the results will be anything but perfect. We learn what works by finding out what doesn't. Thomas Edison failed 1,000 times before inventing the lightbulb; you saw how President Lincoln failed his way to the top; Agatha Christie was rejected for five years before finally finding someone who would publish her books – she now is outsold only by William Shakespeare.

Do you punish yourself and others when they make a mistake? How harsh are you on yourself and others when there's a failure? A leader acknowledges the fault and knows that it brought us one step closer to a solution.

Caring

Whether a leader exhibits all or some of the characteristics we have discussed, without *caring*, we are back to square one and the rampant disinterest for others that mercenaries exhibit. With caring, many mistakes can be made yet the result will still be accomplished. I have no idea what kind of a man Dan Price, CEO of Gravity Payments, is to work for, but I do know he took his role as the head of his company seriously when he read research which showed that a salary of $70,000 a year is the threshold for happiness. Less than that brings anxiety and fear, more than that adds no extra happiness. He cared about his employees enough that he raised the minimum wage at his company to $70,000. His company is still profitable, and he even reduced his own salary to $70,000 from the seven figures it had been. This is a far cry from the CEOs who are making 350 times more than the average worker. Caring about their employees is not on their radar, and what they get are robotic workers who are just there for a paycheck.

A client of mine who had a fairly small fabrication company wanted to grow it and make it more profitable. He had large goals for production and profits, but to my delight, he also said he wanted his staff to be happy.

When generating a vision for how the company will look, what the numbers will be, and how to go about getting there, it is a very different scenario when the owner is interested in his staff instead of just the bottom line.

The project did not take any longer than other similar ones I had taken on with other clients. The goals were met, and one of the high points for my client was not looking at the great numbers, but when he received a huge birthday card signed by each of his twenty-five-plus employees.

Feisty and Fearless Challenge #5:

For the next month, pay attention to the people around you. Notice when you show them that you care: it could be a smile, a word of encouragement or support, or adding a little extra personalization to an email.

Command and Control

While there are some occasions when commanding is appropriate, such as when giving an order in the military or when telling a child not to run into the road, in most situations a command is disempowering. It is the equivalent of saying you are not capable of making a decision or knowing what to do, so I have to tell you and, by the way, you had better obey. There is no room for the person's opinion, input, ideas or feedback. Commanding is wiping one's feet on other people, belittling them, and as with a lack of caring, it results in employees' robotic disengagement. Don't question, just do it. Go to work, collect a paycheck, go home. Thus we have *happy hour* to shrug off the debilitating effect of such an environment. Leading a team includes being firm, but that is different from commanding.

Mercenaries who command don't see people; they only see pawns to be played in their game of winner-takes-all. They care not whether their words or actions hurt or disempower their employees, only that the results are achieved.

There is very little we can control, yet the old definition of leadership suggests that control is one of the elements that make a leader. We cannot control anyone, at least not for very long or very effectively, nor can we control much in the way of outcomes.

This idea flies in the face of Western thinking, which says that everything can be looked at as cause-and-effect: if you do *a*, then *b* will follow. This is basic logic, right? How, then, do we account for genetic mutations? Politicians who defy the pollsters and unexpectedly win (or lose) an election? Or when you create a detailed plan to achieve a result, take the actions and still don't accomplish it? While self-control in the form of discipline can be useful, using control as a style of leadership is the antithesis of empowerment.

Feisty & Fearless Challenge #6:
How often have you been frustrated because you think you should be able to make something happen but it doesn't work out? The next time that happens, stop. Write down what you are trying to do, why you are trying to do it, and what is happening that is thwarting your attempts. It is only by itemizing these things that you can see how you have been approaching the issue. Then you can ask the appropriate questions: are the right actions being taken? Is there something not being done that needs to be? Are the right people assigned? Is more training needed? When you have asked and answered these and other questions, the solution might still be evading you, in which case it might be time to rethink the project.

Give up the illusion of control and see just how much more you will achieve.

Followers

We all have to follow during our lives – our parents, teachers, and bosses. Learning by rote rather than questioning and developing critical thinking is *check-the-box* teaching and learning, and it deprives us of the opportunity to stretch and learn to our full potential. What we learn instead is that we are not valued, that it is better to not make any suggestions or think creatively. Then we have a workforce that will not be the equal of those that figured out how to take us to the moon. With minds locked down, how will we find the solution to climate change, water shortages, or our broken political system?

A workforce of placid *followers* might be easier to manage, but it does not make for a vital, long-lived organization that ventures into new frontiers. Whether the company is a technology-based company, a food manufacturer, or a drug company, its future depends not on merely selling its current products, but on its innovations and ideas for tomorrow. This achievement requires followers who are themselves leaders, employees who are interested in their work and willing to try something different.

Followers of leaders rather than mercenaries know they are valued, their ideas are wanted, and their creativity is encouraged. These followers enjoy going to work, rather than counting the days until their next vacation or wondering if anyone will notice if they call in sick for a day.

Feisty & Fearless Challenge #7:

What can be improved in the organization you work for? Is there a process that doesn't work that you can suggest how to streamline? A way to market a product to a particular group that you feel is not being addressed by the company? Be bold, and find a way to bring this to the attention of the person you report to, or the person you feel would sponsor it through.

Credit

Have you noticed that men want credit for everything? Whether at home or on the job, every little thing they do they want to make sure everyone knows they did it. Women just want to get the job done. Chinese philosophers long ago noted that a great leader is one who, when the job is accomplished, is in the background, with the people on the team taking the credit. I, like many women, have sometimes been happy to let the men take the credit and receive the praise because I would rather keep the relationship. While very noble, this hurts our careers and earning power, as we are less likely to pursue promotions or competitive projects. So ladies, tone up the muscle of speaking up about your accomplishments – even the little ones – because lots of those little ones add up to big ones and will move you faster along your career path.

Feisty & Fearless Challenge #8:

Time to write again. This time make a list of things you have accomplished in the last year. Big accomplishments will immediately come to mind, but think about the little things too. Maybe you encouraged one of your direct reports, and she had a breakthrough and gave her team the ideas they had been trying to find; or you got your teenager to clean out her room. Think about last week, then last month and they will trigger those you hardly bothered to note earlier on – like the time you were actually heard in the meeting where you were the only woman.

When you have the list, sit down, maybe pour yourself a glass of wine, and savor what you have done. This is great for building confidence and short-circuiting the self-doubts that come into our heads.

Next, look the list over again and decide which ones need to be acknowledged by someone else. At work this is so important because it can be the difference between being stuck in the same position or moving up. It is essential to let it be known that you are accomplished. Take this on, and then make it a habit. It is not bragging; it is merely making sure your talents are acknowledged and fixed in the minds of people who will be looking for upcoming stars to promote or assign to special projects.

Being Right

Wanting to be right is very much a human tendency. A leader, however, will give up being right to sustain a relationship, to get the job done, or to achieve a desired result. I remember being asked long ago, "Do you want to be right, or do you want to get the result?" It brought me up short because until then, I thought it very important to be right and to defend myself to the end if I knew I was right. The problem with insisting on being right, is that it usually means the other person is wrong, and when we insist on being right, it gives that person no way to save face and consider that there may be a different way to look at things. Mercenaries don't care about the other person. They will be relentless in their insistence on being right, no matter the cost.

There are times, however, when being right and standing firm is the mark of a leader. When people told me I would never get a women's commission in Glendale, I knew they were wrong so I continued to drive the team to its successful conclusion.

Feisty & Fearless Challenge #9:

The next time you want to argue for your position on a topic, take a second to consider whether this will be beneficial in the long term, whether it's something important to you, or whether you just want to be right.

Formal Education

As we have already seen, brain power is often thought to be a prerequisite of leadership. This just is not so. There are leaders who would not do well on institutionalized tests. There used to be less emphasis on advanced degrees, yet still we have some pretty impressive leaders: the baker who figures out how to make pastry that melts in your mouth; the parent who raises a child to be a caring, compassionate and loving adult; a single mother who builds a successful company – these are all leaders in their own way. They use their hearts as much as their brains.

Do you have a master's degree or a doctorate? Congratulations. That took a lot of hard work (not to say a whole lot of money). Now your opportunity is to use both the education and the critical thinking that you learned on the way to attaining your degree. If you finished high school and are wondering if you should have continued on to college, think about a different question. Ask yourself what really drives you, what delights you and what frustrations you face. You might discover the answer to the question of where you need to focus your attention.

One degree, or several, does not automatically make you a leader. Perhaps you have started or are thinking of starting a business. That takes a lot of work and a whole lot of leadership, but it doesn't necessarily require a formal education.

If, however, you want to be a leader in a field that requires academic credentials, then your choice will be to go back to school.

Standards

Who is to say that one leader is better than another? By what standards are we measuring them? Maybe that is the only question to ask – what are the standards?

How do we look at standards to determine which ones to use? Rather than using a moral filter of good and bad, I like to characterize standards as *workable* and *non-workable*. Even when we use these standards we still need to identify criteria that define what is considered workable and what is not.

We need to realize that to generalize is to miss the point. A *one-size-fits-all* theory of leadership does not work and applies to no one. Over the last hundred years there have been many books written about leadership, many relating to just a few leadership theories. The vast majority have been written by and for men and only recently has there been any written with a consideration of women as leaders.

At conferences around the globe, theorists, researchers, consultants, managers and leaders of all kinds are pointing in the same direction: away from command and control, force and power; domination and male-only leadership. Instead they are pointing to more humane, communicative, compassionate and inclusive leadership standards.

This does not mean that when decisive action is needed, leaders will not step up; neither does it mean that leadership decisions are going to be made by committee. What it does mean is that women must and will be more involved in leadership, from the family level up to the national and global levels.

No longer can the stereotypical male characteristics of leading and decision-making alone be considered sufficient when evidence showing otherwise is so bountiful. The other half of the world, the female half, brings a distinct perspective that is as important and needed as men's in reaching decisions and creating solutions to the world's problems, both major and minor.

6

ABOUT LEADERSHIP

How old do you have to be to be a leader? Twenty? Thirty? Fifty? In talking with leaders, I found that many of them were leaders as children. Some as young as four or five, so there really is no age limit. That doesn't mean if you did not take on any kind of leadership as a child you must not be able to be a leader. It is never too late, or too early. When you're ready, you're ready.

When I was twentysomething I heard in the news about young women and men, some in their teens, who already had performed some great feat of leadership: addressing the United Nations General Assembly; mobilizing their whole student body to provide school supplies for a school in a developing country; or coming together against racism. I felt I had missed the boat; I was a failure and my life was worthless; I was all washed up. I found out later that leadership can be picked up at any age or any stage of life.

The Honorable Patty Murray, U.S. senator for the state of Washington took on leadership in her thirties; Rosa Parks was 42 when she refused to go to the back of the bus; at 33 actress Bette Davis became the first female president of the Academy of Motion Picture Arts and Sciences; Susan B. Anthony, leader of the effort that resulted in passage of the 19th Amendment to the United States Constitution, giving women the vote, was 49 when she co-founded the National Woman Suffrage Association. Examples and role models are endless. At every age, there is someone who stands up and declares it her time to take the reins and lead the way.

What a leader is and how to define it is not going to be settled for all time on these pages. However, as we learn and grow and succeed and suffer setbacks, the need to transform and grow and amend what we now call leadership is essential.

Do Men Make Better Leaders?

In a recent study by the Pew Research Center, both men and women say there is no difference in who can be leaders, men or women. This is a positive shift because earlier studies had shown that both men and women felt men make better leaders. The consultancy Zenger Folkman examined 45,000 corporate leaders and determined that women were more effective than men in three leadership pillars: getting things done, being role models, and delivering results. A 2014 international survey showed over a quarter of the companies with a financial performance in the top 20 percent had female leaders, and those companies that performed at the bottom 20 percent had only 19 percent women at the helm.

In Lima, Peru, a field study by Sabrina Karim found that public perceptions of whether bribery was a major problem among traffic police had plummeted in 2012, compared with fourteen years earlier. The change came after recruiting 2,500 women to patrol the streets.

A separate public opinion survey showed overwhelming approval for the job done by female traffic officers. From the point of view of the female traffic police, Karim, now a doctoral candidate at Emory University, found that almost all of those surveyed thought the presence of women on the force had reduced corruption, and two-thirds believed women were less corrupt.

If there were 250 female CEOs of the Fortune 500 companies, we would see more women in the executive ranks, a supposition that breaks the myth that when women achieve higher status, they do not reach down to help other women up. A study out in 2015 in the UK reports that when women are at the helm of a large corporation, it actually increases the probability of more women being promoted rather than reducing the chances of other women rising up through the ranks.

What would change if half the U.S. senators and members of the House of Representatives were women, and twenty-five governors of the states were women? Might there be different thinking about who is a leader with that kind of balance? I suspect so.

In the meantime, I ask that you step up to the plate and be the leader you are and can be. We need you. Women are a long way from being half the leaders in any walk of life, and it is up to each of us to help change that. Whether you are leading your family or a group of coworkers, or reaching beyond your immediate circle, your stepping up pushes everyone up.

Half the Sky, a book by Sheryl WuDunn and Nicholas Kristof, speaks to the benefit of everyone when girls and women are educated and are allowed to be the natural leaders they are. There are men who want to oppress and suppress women, but there are many others who see how they and their children, as well as others in their towns, villages and cities, benefit when women come into their own.

Do You Have to Be Born a Leader?

I come from a country where queens and kings say it is only their progeny who will be, and are, fit to succeed to the throne. Does this make them leaders? History tells us otherwise. Geneticists have yet to announce that there is a gene for leadership.

What then is the difference between those we call *born leaders* and the rest of us? Listening to the leaders I interviewed, it became clear that becoming a leader is a choice we make. Either there is a gap of leadership that needs filling, as with Leigh Adams who raised her hand, or an opportunity such as was presented to Maia Mossé to lead the team of volunteer interpreters to staff hospital visits. Both could have made the choice to walk away or to decline the opportunity, but instead they chose to take it on. In both cases, they report they had no idea how to do what they were being asked to do.

It doesn't even have had to occur to you that you want to be a leader. Sometimes the decision to be a leader, to take on a leadership role, is a choice you make midstream. Maybe you agreed to take on a project at work, for instance, not realizing what was being asked of you was to lead a team, creating the vision for the project and then inspiring the team to complete it. Or maybe it happens as it did with me, when the idea of a women's commission sounded like something that was needed in the city of Glendale. I started talking to some people, doing some research, and before I could say "Fabulous Feminist," I was in the middle of a major project with everyone looking to me to make it happen.

On any day at any time of our life, we can make a decision that alters the direction of our life, sometimes dramatically, sometimes subtly. Thus it is with a decision to become a leader. It may be that your life is moving in what you consider the wrong direction, and one day you say, "enough." Or perhaps your life is wonderful, you have achieved your goals, the circumstances of your life – your home and family – are all you could wish for. It occurs to you that you have more to give and contribute, and it is time to take that on.

Feisty & Fearless Challenge #10:
We have different rites of passage given to us by our cultures and religions; this is one you can give yourself. You can declare, "Today I am a Leader."

"Now what?" or "How do I do that?" might be the next thought that pops up in your mind. I recommend you then start a new file on your computer or tablet, and write down whatever comes. This will most likely be a vision you have of what you really want to do; or maybe you'll come up with a whole bunch of negatives about why you think you cannot be a leader. Both results are useful.

If you have the vision, then you are on your way. Start taking action, and watch as it unfolds. If it is the negatives that come to mind, what you have is a list of the first tasks to be added to your action plan. These are things to be written down, reviewed, and addressed. Some of what you write down will be merely self-doubt that you can let go; other things will be specific and useful. As an example, it could be that you need to take a parenting class to be more confident leading your family, or join Toastmasters so you can be more comfortable speaking in front of groups and making presentations, or go back to school to finish a degree or earn a certification.

Once you get started, the path will open up in front you. Go for it!

Do Leaders Need a Title?

We often think titles such as Chief Executive Officer, Executive Director, or Prime Minister denote leadership. Not always. I was amazed when, as a management consultant, I would meet people in management positions who knew little or nothing about how to lead. Usually they were people who had been doing a good job and were promoted. They were given a title and very little training, yet they were expected to manage people and produce a set of results. When they achieved the results, they were promoted to the next level, again without training. Thus it went until they made it all the way through the ranks to the executive level.

They had to learn to manage, yet leadership was hardly mentioned. But at the executive level, leadership, not management, is their most important job. With so much history and experience as a manager, it is doubly difficult to learn to be a leader, so although there are leadership programs aimed at this level, they are rarely enough to break new executives out of the box of management and ignite real leadership.

The title then can be misleading. Behind CEO, CIO, COO, CMO and so on can be a manager who may have surprised himself he has risen this far, but who now must defend and protect his position at all costs. Decisions focus on self-protection and aggrandizement rather than on employees, community, or constituents.

Look around the world at the presidents and prime ministers who are corrupt, who line their pockets while their constituents, the people they are supposed to be leading, are living in abject poverty. Not two weeks after the massive earthquake in Nepal left thousands dead and hundreds of thousands of people homeless, reports came out that the country's leaders were keeping the aid money instead of distributing it to those in need and for whom the money was intended. Is this what it means to be a leader? I think not.

Titles of the kinds of leaders this book proposes include mother, artist, blind teacher, author, teenager, janitor. Leaders are all around us, women and men, girls and boys, who have taken on the responsibility of making something happen.

To be clear, I am not saying that anyone with the title of President, Prime Minister or CEO cannot be a leader. What I am saying is that there is something other than the title that makes a leader. Leadership starts from the inside out. Do you have a vision? Does that vision contribute to the many? Does it harm anyone or the planet? Do you care? Or if you are honest, are you just delighted to have your ego buffed up, your paycheck raised and some nice perks coming your way? Which kind of leader will you choose to be? The richer one will be the leader who has the satisfaction of a job well done in making a difference for people. Here are a couple of great examples.

Our office-building janitor, a Latina who looks like she is built to last and who will flash her warm smile at anyone interested in acknowledging her, spent twenty years working from 6:00 p.m. to 2:00 a.m. while raising her family. Her son went to college and now is a teacher, has a family himself and contributes to his community. I am sure he would agree that his mother is indeed a leader and a great role model for him and his siblings.

Rafi Manoukian is a CPA, a father of three and a former councilmember and mayor of Glendale, California. Rafi took his position of representing his constituents seriously. He didn't just sit in the council chambers each week to hear whoever came and spoke before the council. He went out into the community and invited anyone and everyone to have a cup of coffee and talk to him about the city and any needs, suggestions or complaints they had.

Feisty & Fearless Challenge #11:

It's not hard to be a leader; it is just a choice. How would you describe your style of leadership? What are some instances when you have taken on being a leader? When was the first time?

Making the list is important because not only will it boost your confidence, but also it can be useful the next time you interview for a job.

7

STORIES FROM THE FIELD

When Linda Lazar, CEO of IrishLemons, a web development company, first suggested that I write a book, she had in mind that I write down the stories I had told her. Below is a sampling, followed by stories of some women with whom I have been impressed, women who are authentic in their leadership and embody the principles in this book.

I hope you will indulge me as I tell you this next story because it was a defining moment for me. With this accomplishment, I could finally accept that I am a leader.

Getting my breakfast one morning early in 2002, my thoughts for the day were interrupted with, "Wow, take a look at this," Barry said. "Here's a list of the top salaries at the City of Los Angeles." As I looked through the list my attention was immediately drawn to the person at the *bottom* of the list: Paula Petrotta, Executive Director of the Los Angeles Commission on the Status of Women. First, I was incensed that she was at the bottom of the list. Second, this was the first I had heard of a Commission on the Status of Women. Intrigued, I found their phone number and called them up.

When I received a packet of information from them I was delighted to see the work being done to root out and work on segments of my half – the female half – of the population that needed some attention. I found out, for instance, that the number of girls being incarcerated had jumped dramatically over the previous few years, and that a large percentage of teenage girls feel pressured to have sex with their boyfriends. That reminded me of my own teenage years. Nothing has changed on that front I guess.

Normally, after reading such material, I would have tossed it as I really don't like to hold onto too much paper and create clutter in my office. For some reason, however, I hung onto it, telling myself that I wasn't sure why, but I knew I would want this for something that wasn't yet clear to me.

Fast-forward a couple of months to the first Thursday morning in May, when Barry and I had ducked out of the office for a few minutes to run to the Glendale Farmer's Market. The mayor was set up for an hour of *Ask the Mayor.* Barry stopped to talk to him about a couple of things, and as I listened a question bubbled up and out of my mouth. "Mayor Manoukian," I asked, "Does the City of Glendale have a Commission on the Status of Women?" "No," the mayor answered, "Do we need one?"

As he asked that question, it was as if the globe tilted a little on its axis. Something shifted. "I'm not sure," I said lamely, "maybe." He went on: "Well, if you think we need one, put together a proposal and I will make sure it gets in front of the council." "OK," I replied, "thanks Mr. Mayor."

I was looking to get involved in the community and give back and I knew I had found what I was looking for. My mind was quiet and storming all at the same time. On the one hand, I knew I had the challenge I had been seeking. On the other hand, I wondered if I was nuts, if I had taken on just a little more than I could chew, given that I had not a clue about how to do this. I thought back on other projects I had taken on, other times when I had raised my hand and said I would do something and feeling immediately like I had lost my mind. As somewhat of an adrenaline junkie, along with the fear clutching at my stomach, the little girl in me was going yahoo! What fun! This is going to be a heck-of-a ride!

Glendale was the third largest city in the County of Los Angeles, with a checkered history – such as sundown laws that meant if you were not white, you had to be out of town by 6:00 p.m. or have a letter from a white person as to why you were still in town. It also had been the home of the John Birch Society, all in all not the most tolerant of burgs. I wanted to stand up for women. OK then. Nothing like a little extra challenge to make it a tasty morsel to bite off.

Glendale is a little better today, with a diverse population and an annual festival called UnityFest celebrating differences. Armenians, Hispanics, Latinos, Asians, African Americans and Caucasians living together, mostly in harmony. Can't you just hear the birds singing, see the nannies smiling and the children laughing? I know, let's not get too carried away. As with most other things in life, scratch the surface and things might look a little different. At the time there was a lawsuit brought against the city by four female law enforcement officers for sexual harassment, which the police officers won. A gynecologist who works in Glendale, upon hearing what I was doing, confided in me that there was a cultural problem of immigrant women having twenty or thirty abortions as their form of birth control. One of the women running for city council at the time asked me if I knew how many women had actually sat on the city council in the ninety-seven years Glendale had been a city. I did not. "Four," she said. "Four women in almost one hundred years."

I had the answer to the mayor's question, "Do we need a Women's Commission?" With only minimal investigation, I had started to uncover some real disparities. Clearly, this was only the tip of the iceberg. I knew I would find more.

I visited women's commissions in Pasadena and in Santa Monica, and it was at the Santa Monica Women's Commission that I met Kelly Hayes-Raitt, a commissioner and board member of the Association of the California Commissions for Women. She urged me to attend the annual meeting of the association, where I had the privilege of meeting staff and members of women's commissions from around the state of California. I heard of their struggles and their successes. I read their reports and studies they had completed showing the inequities between men and women that exist in so many areas of our lives. I wept, and yet was called more fervently into action. I knew I had to get the city council to create the women's commission. There were one hundred thousand women and girls in Glendale that needed me to get this done. I took on Susan B. Anthony's mantra, *Failure is not an option.*

Humbled, empowered and ready to take on anyone and anybody, I returned to Glendale from the association meeting with my sleeves rolled up. Where can I speak? To which group? At what meeting? I had to get the word out far and wide. I met with Mayor Rafi Manoukian again, who told me that if I wanted to ensure my success, I needed to get as much of the community behind me as possible. I was on the right track.

As momentum built, a team of women and men formed to help. What can we do? Who can we tell? From each of these people I heard a story. Some of the men told of their respect for their single mothers who worked so hard to raise them; women confided in me of discrimination and harassment they had experienced or had witnessed in their family or with friends. Professional women angrily talked of pay inequities.

As this effort took form and the list of people and groups endorsing the formation of the commission grew, I began to be asked, "Why are you doing this?" "What do you want out of this?" "What's your agenda?" People were suspicious.

I was amazed. I was so on fire with doing something that I thought would make a difference, would do more than just raise some money for a good cause, that I was offended and more than a little hurt. The first time I was asked this, it stopped me in my tracks. Why do we ever do anything for someone else? For one thing, we do it because it makes us feel good, and I was feeling terrific as I watched this take shape.

"Don't listen to them," Ellen Snortland, a local author and columnist said encouragingly to me; "they just wish they had the gumption to do what you are doing." I tried listening to her advice, but I must admit that each time I heard it, I winced.

I used my knowledge and experience from consulting and kicked things into high gear: I made an action plan; brought together a team to guide and advise me; set up a communication system to keep in touch with everyone; garnered endorsements from elected officials; found more residents and groups to engage; solicited media coverage; and began writing the proposal.

I felt alive. I had found a passion inside of me that I had not had for a very long time. The Energizer bunny had nothing on me as I checked things off my list, made another phone call, scheduled another speaking engagement, wrote another email.

As the date to present the proposal to the city council came close, although I still caught the quizzical look of someone wondering what was in it for me, I was also aware of something else. I heard women in particular being glad and hopeful that maybe, just maybe, there would be a voice for them in the government of our city. I heard their hope.

On January 14, 2003, our team gathered at City Hall, downstairs from the council chambers. With people coming from work to support us, they needed something to eat. OK, I know this feeds (excuse the pun) the notion that we women are nurturers, but hey, people would be hungry. We set up tables and served refreshments. It was alive; there was electricity in the air. This was a historic party that the people of Glendale wanted to be a part of. Elena Ong was there representing the California State Commission on the Status of Women; Kelly Hayes-Raitt had spent two hours in rush-hour traffic to come, representing the Santa Monica Women's Commission; Olivia Rodriguez represented the Los Angeles County Women's Commission. Representatives from other elected officials were present. Ellen Snortland, who had written two columns about us in the *Pasadena Weekly* was there. The late retired Police Chief Bruce Philpott was there.

We had wanted to make sure the city council knew that there were lots of us, so we had made big yellow buttons that had the word "WOMEN" in bold letters across them and "Glendale Commission on the Status of Women" around the edge, and we gave everyone a badge to wear as they arrived.

I had my PowerPoint presentation, along with a binder for each council member. I wore my yellow button.

When it was my turn, I walked nervously up to the podium knowing I had all these people supporting me – and counting on me. I had better not blow it!

"Mr. Mayor, Councilmembers, Staff," I began, and continued for the ten minutes they had allotted to me. My mind had stilled, I was focused. I followed my script. I let my heart guide me. Following me, one by one, the other speakers made the case for the commission, answering questions from council members and being clear that this was the right thing to do.

We got the vote, four out of five, and we had only needed three. Time to breathe.

That's what we had done in Glendale, and now we, the women of Glendale, would have a voice in the city government.

Feisty & Fearless Challenge # 12:

What project is there in your home, at work, church, or community group that you have seen needs to be taken on but which you have been unsure of embracing for some reason? If you took it on, who could you ask or invite to help, support, partner with or mentor you to make it happen?

An Impossible Situation – Defying the Laws of Physics
What would you have done?

Several years ago I was faced with a decision that was excruciatingly painful. I needed to be in two places at the same time, and as the laws of physics preclude that, I had to find some other solution.

To give you some background, my consulting business was doing well and growing. I was in London visiting family, and I never missed a chance to network for new business. While I was talking with my cousin Murray at a family gathering, I found out he owned a computer company in Cambridge and had recently been considering how to grow the business, build a more cohesive team, and develop leaders.

Instantly I switched into sales mode, asking him for more information about his company and what he really wanted. We talked some more, and on my return to Los Angeles I put together a proposal of what I could do to help. We set a date for me to spend time with him and his management team, followed by a day's workshop with all the staff, closing the company down so everyone could attend.

We had come up with an aggressive set of goals, so my preparation had to be thorough and fine-tuned. Meanwhile, as all this preparation had been going on, phone calls back and forth with my mother included news of my beloved grandma Bella who at ninety-something was now quite sick and fading fast.

As I was trying to relax on the flight to London, I allowed myself to consider something that had been nagging at the back of my mind: the possibility that my grandma might die while I was there. How would I handle the logistics of that? I knew that I could handle it emotionally, so that wasn't my concern.

When I arrived at the company I noticed a decided buzz; everyone was very excited about what was going to happen the following day. They all knew I was the consultant who had been flown in from Los Angeles and that the company was being closed down for a whole day, something that had never happened before. Clearly this was really important.

With this excitement, I felt the weight of responsibility become a little heavier. I met with Murray and with each of the managers. Halfway through the morning I was summoned to Murray's office for a phone call, this being at a time before I had a cell phone. My heart sank, knowing what I would hear. "Hello, this is Pauline," I said. "Hello dear," my mother said, "grandma just died." "I am so sorry," I replied. The other shoe was about to drop; I knew that my family would be strictly following the Jewish laws that insist on burial within twenty-four hours. "The funeral is set for tomorrow afternoon at 1:00 p.m.," my mother continued. I felt like I had been punched in the stomach and thought I might faint.

Here I was in London, and my dear grandma had died and was about to be buried on the very day that this company had made elaborate plans to work with me. I was in quite a pickle; how could I be with my family and this company at the same time?

When I got back to my mother's house, I burned the phone wires back to Los Angeles. I wanted someone to tell me what to do because I felt incapable of dealing with this situation. My mother of course expected me to be at the funeral. There was no question in her mind.

How do I not disrespect my family, and not let Murray and his company down?

I finally decided that somehow I would do both: attend the funeral *and* give the company a great day. I spent hours redesigning the work so I could take the time necessary to attend at least part of the funeral. Although I came up with what seemed to be a workable solution, I had my doubts.

I slept fitfully, still not sure of how and whether the following day was going to work.

When I arrived there the next morning, everyone was anxious to get started. Phones were turned to voicemail, and we began. They turned out to be a very receptive group and it moved along well. I was immersed in the work and results were happening. All too soon it was time for me to leave for the race to the cemetery. I set them up for the exercises I had designed for them. There was enough for them to do while I was gone.

My history of fast driving, together with the loose speed limits on the English freeways, came in handy that day as I sped my way from Cambridge to the cemetery. I arrived in time to be with my mother for a few minutes.

After hugs with Mum and some family members, as well as a few tears, I hopped back into my rental car and sped back to Cambridge.

The team was almost finished with the work I had left them and were ready to report what they had designed in my absence.

I picked up the reins and completed the work of the day, at the end of which Murray expressed his appreciation for a job well done. He was feeling more positive about his company and its future than he had in a long time.

I learned a major lesson that day: "either/or" can be a trap, a dead-end. Even when it looks like there are only two options from which to choose, it is possible to step back and put the two options and the whole situation in a different perspective, providing the potential of a previously unseen third option without the drawbacks of either of the other two. I have used this countless times since.

Feisty & Fearless Challenge #13:
For the next week, catch yourself every time there seem to be just two solutions to a problem or issue. This can be as simple as

whether you eat out or stay in and cook. Ask yourself if, indeed, there could be another solution. This could be related somehow to one of the two options, or it might be something totally different. Make your decision only after having reviewed all the options – even the ones that seem impossible or ridiculous. It is sometimes out of the ridiculous ideas that a viable one emerges.

Leadership = Empowerment

This story is from a time when I was working long hours and wondering if there were parts of my life I was missing. I have often found answers to questions I hardly knew I was asking in a variety of different places. Small children are very inquisitive. When they are told something, they want to know why; when they see something happening, they want to know how it happened, will it happen again, can they have it, and so on. It seems that we lose some of this inquisitiveness as we learn to toe the line and fit in – to be *nice* and do things right. To grow and expand and fulfill our dreams, we have to pick up those questions again. As you can see from Kimberly's story (which follows), the about-face she made in her career had a big impact on me, and her story would pop up in my mind every time I found myself working rather than doing something enriching or fun.

While networking one morning I met Kimberly, a spokesperson for an international direct relief agency for whom I had consulted. We immediately hit it off and agreed to meet and get to know each other better.

Later that week over steaming lattes, she told me her powerful and poignant story about how she quit a high-powered, European country-hopping top executive marketing job and returned to Los Angeles to work with a nonprofit relief agency.

Kimberly told me that while she was a marketing executive running around Europe, she worked all the time, was under constant pressure to produce, and although she enjoyed her work, she did not have a life outside of work. If you have travelled on business, you know it is a far cry from being a tourist and enjoying the sights. Mostly it is airplanes, hotel rooms, office buildings, and food on the run.

At the end of one particular project she decided to break loose and use some of her vacation time, something she had not done in a while. Towards the end of a Kenyan safari, she was in a small village in a remote part of the country. The people in the village were warm and friendly, and from Kimberly's perspective the village overall was impoverished, with very little in the way of modern conveniences. She was saying goodbye after having enjoyed her time among them, when a woman who was a little older, a little rounder, and who had a warm smile and a ready laugh gave Kimberley a hug, looked into her eyes and said how sorry she was to see Kimberley's sadness.

This was not what she expected to hear; after all she had a great job, a beautiful home and money in the bank. In that moment, however, Kimberly saw that the person with the riches was this woman with the wide smile and warm eyes who had so little in the way of material things and so much in relationships and enjoyment of life. Kimberley was the one who was impoverished. The next day she submitted her resignation, feeling lighter and freer than she had in years and clear that a new life was now open to her.

Feisty & Fearless Challenge # 14:

Are you working in the field about which you are passionate? Or are you just making a living? Is there something else you would rather be doing in your life – join AmeriCorps, take a course or finish a degree, move to a different part of the country – or to a different country? Take a few minutes and write down what's been at the back of your mind with no thoughts or judgments about whether or not you will take it on, or whether you have the resources or support you need.

You may be ready to jump in and take it on, but you may not. If you are not, don't worry. This is a start and it begins the process. The seed will have been planted.

Out of My Comfort Zone - Running for City Council

Has anyone ever asked you to do something, take on a project that seemed so far out of your capabilities, so unlike anything you had ever done before that you hardly considered it? That's how I felt when I was asked to run for a seat on the Glendale City Council.

Many of the people who had helped me get the women's commission established were urging me to run for the city council. I definitely wanted to see the number of women increase from the historical four. Should I? Could I? Being an elected official had always seemed a little intimidating, but now serving on the women's commission, it seemed more achievable. I was also now much more involved in the community, so this seemed a logical next step, if a little daunting.

I moved forward. I looked for the positives and the parts of it that seemed to fit me: I liked talking to strangers and had been marketing my business for twenty years, so I knew a little about getting the word out and had a fair amount of name recognition. I was not afraid of competition, which was just as well because there were lots of others also running for the three open seats. Plus I wanted to make a difference. Surely these were the main ingredients for success.

I went to a training course and as experience is always useful, I met with a couple of women who had held elective office to get their take on what a campaign was like, what to be sure to do and perhaps just as important, what things to avoid. I also was interested in their keys to success.

I knew that organizational skills and effective time management were critical so, as there was an enormous amount of work to be done in the campaign, I started by scheduling my days to ensure I took care of myself. It went like this:

Up at 6:00 a.m. No appointments or meetings until 10:00 a.m. This gave me time for my daily rituals, including exercising, to take care of myself before jumping into the meetings, calls, proposals and debates in front of me. It worked. I felt energetic and ready to take on the work each day. For the next four months I spoke at candidate forums, grew a list of supporters, raised money and garnered endorsements.

I was not elected. Just as I noted at the beginning of the book, sometimes as leaders we fail; we miss the mark. I was disappointed, of course, as were my supporters. Fair enough, time to move on and learn from the experience. I took the time to make note of what I had indeed learned from this experience, knowing that these lessons would stand me in good stead in the future.

While I am talking about the political realm, I have read about a great example of leadership. Ada Colau, the new mayor of Barcelona, Spain. Ms. Colau, who is not a politician, won election against seasoned politicians. She did that because a fire was lit inside her. When the recession hit in 2008 and she saw so many families lose their homes through foreclosure, she knew she had to do something. She founded an organization that fought to stop evictions and was fueled by her passion, protesting against the banks, who she felt were wrong, and the government, which just stood by and did nothing. She just did what she felt she needed to do, and many people agreed, sweeping her into power as the person who would fight for them and their communities.

Whatever you want to do and have the passion for, it is worth taking the risk. Just as her supporters swept Ms. Colau into power, so people will follow you when you lead from your heart, not just from your head.

Stories of More Feisty and Fearless Nice Girls

I have included these stories because they exemplify the values and characteristics spoken of earlier in the book. I hope some of them speak to you. The words of a few of them – Claudette, Sharon, Ellen and Shelby – are verbatim.

Leigh Adams – Learning by Doing

When conducting a leadership training program for 50/50 Leadership, at each session we invited community leaders to come tell their story. I have to admit to being very amused at the juxtaposition of two leaders who came to speak: first was a buttoned up corporate type who not only followed the rules, but insisted that it was the only way to get ahead. She was followed by an artist, Leigh Adams, one of the most truly authentic people I have ever met. She is the antithesis of corporate, however. Leigh wears flowing clothes, and her longish grey hair is liberally enhanced with purple highlights, into which she sports a flower behind one ear. As well as setting up the talk she gave to our trainees at 50/50 Leadership, I have worked with Leigh on team-building programs in business. Managers have been initially shocked and dubious when I have brought her in. Her appearance accomplishes what otherwise can take hours: workshop participants are immediately exploded out of their comfortable ways of thinking, jolted out of what they have previously known a leader to look like. Without opening her mouth, attendees are out of their normal thinking patterns, saving her much time in being able to get to the work she is hired to do.

Leigh is a leader, an artist and a teacher, and has a grin that envelops and engages everyone who comes close, aged five to ninety-five.

Of the many stories Leigh tells about her leadership successes, her passion for empowering children has her pluck from her memory stash the time she lead twenty-five children in a camping program from the private school where she taught.

Mostly, children show up at camping trips to be entertained and be the recipients of the adults' hard work in planning and preparation. Leigh knew that underestimating the students by not having them be a part of all that goes into putting on a camping trip deprives them of the growth and empowerment available when they do the preparation themselves.

With Leigh's guidance, the students planned and implemented the whole thing: what to eat and the shopping list to make it all; how to cook it and the utensils needed; how to store the food and how much it cost. They created a schedule of who would do the shopping, the cooking, and the cleaning. The students decided on the activities they wanted on the trip, such as hiking, fishing, or swimming. They discovered what was available in and around their campsite, thought about training needed and considered whether every student would be able to participate. This planning became a semester-long course that led up to the actual camping trip, enriching and educating them, as well as giving them a new confidence and sense of themselves and their abilities. This was so successful in making a difference for these students that when Leigh sees them now as adults, she always gets hugs and accolades from them, many of them saying that it was a turning point in their lives. Isn't a teacher a leader? Just as a mother's role is profoundly important, so is the role of a teacher.

More recently, Leigh had been volunteering at the Los Angeles County Arboretum and saw a need for them to have an Artist in Residence. They had never had one, and Leigh knew this was something missing. She took it on and went about making it happen. Once installed, she took on a project that would be public art created partly with the help of children. She created a snake-shaped path, one thousand feet long and studded with mosaic pieces, each of which was made by a different group of children from around Los Angeles County. Visitors to the Arboretum now come specifically to walk the snake.

Leigh understands the need for sustainability in landscaping, both for the homeowners of Los Angeles County and for the huge spaces of the Arboretum. So she not only created a lush, beautiful, water-sipping and retaining garden around her house, but also worked hard and long until she convinced the management at the Arboretum to design and install such a space. The Arboretum garden is now a model for communities throughout Southern California and beyond.

Leigh's flexibility and fluidity show up not only in her attire, but also in her work. She sees a need and steps into it, using her creativity and her many talents, adding knowledge as needed.

Adora Svitak – Child Leader

I came across Adora Svitak through TED, the website whose tagline and mission is: "Ideas worth spreading." Adora was twelve years old when she spoke to a group of several hundred executives, philanthropists and other successful people at the TED conference in 2010. She delivered the speech "What Adults Can Learn from Kids" and since has received over 3.3 million views. By the age of seven she was a prolific short story writer and blogger and has spoken about literacy to groups around the United States. Leadership knows no age. Two, 22 or 102, we can be leaders when we choose to be. It is a choice. When the opportunity arises, we can step up to it, or we can let the opportunity pass. Leadership is an "inside job." It is not dependent on your age or your circumstances, just whether you are ready and willing to take the actions that are called for.

Have you used your age, that you are too young or too old, to hold you back? Hopefully by now you are realizing you can erase that reason for not taking on your dreams.

Mothers – Our First and Primary Role Models

What greater leadership role is there than being a mother? Despite the fact that women are so denigrated, demeaned, under-valued, discriminated against, oppressed, and suppressed, we nonetheless are given the role of nurturing and educating our children. Mother's Day in the United States is the biggest day of the year for flowers, Sunday brunch, and phone calls. That tells us how important a role we play in the lives of our children. Children may or may not like their mothers. They may be frustrated with their mom or see her as a dinosaur in her thinking, but when all is said and done, they respect her. There is a bond between mother and child that is unmatched. In our culture today it is mothers who are largely responsible for shaping children so that they can become contributing members of society, or not. What a responsibility. The future rests with mothers.

Styles of parenting abound, and like other types of leadership, there is no one size or style that fits all, or one that is the best. Caring and commitment to a child's well-being are what every child needs from at least one person. Anything more is icing on the cupcake.

Ria Severance – Therapist and Mother

Despite the professional kudos Ria Severance, a licensed therapist and executive coach receives from her work with clients and in the community, it is her role as a mother of which she is most proud. *Figuring out how to empathize and empower my kids, knowing and respecting my limits and theirs, without beating the crap out of them* is Ria's somewhat self-deprecating but refreshingly honest view of what it takes to be a mom. It reminds me that we are all human and no matter how well we are doing at leading, there will be days when we feel like doing something very "unleader-like." I understand; Barry tells me all the time that my frustration level is really low, so whether it is children, computers or bad customer service, my default position would be to let out my frustration on the computer or the poor woman on the phone in India, which would only create yet another problem rather than solving the one at hand. I try to avoid taking the default.

Ria is the selfless person everyone wants in the community because she will always seek out and find something that needs to be made, fixed or created, and will become the leader in making it happen.

She readily accepts that she doesn't have a halo over her head, and this has made her a great role model for her children. By seeing that their mother isn't perfect in every way, they have room to be the imperfect humans they are. Ria's daughter, Maia Mossé, is a clear indication of Ria's success and when asked who her most impactful role model has been, it is her mother that she identifies.

Maia Mossé – Starting Early and Continuing Her Leadership

Her willowy figure and an easy if somewhat shy smile immediately endeared me to Maia when we first met during her freshman year at high school. She was still only nineteen when I interviewed her, and I was hardly surprised to hear that her first shot at leadership came at around age five, when she was at a McDonald's with her mother. Not content to just play, she brought the other kids together and had them sing to their parents.

As a freshman at Stanford University, she showed herself to be her mother's daughter: committed, selfless and determined to make a difference. Maia directed sixty people in a pre-med organization coordinating interns and interpreters, and figuring out how to organize them in going to a local hospital. *It is so much bigger than me*, she said, and it is benefiting others by helping to increase the efficiency in the emergency room. In 2015, Maia received Stanford's Community Partnership Award for her work.

Kacee – Singing Her Heart Out

I met Kelly Clanton, better known by her stage name of Kacee, when she moved into the apartment next door to us. Curly red hair only slightly tamed, a nose ring and an *I dare you* attitude came with the warm smile of greeting. She fits the part she plays in New York of the late Janis Joplin. Making a living as a singer without being a star is quite rare, but it's something that Kacee has accomplished and of which she is understandably proud. She gets satisfaction from those *small, amazing moments*. Backstage, for instance, she is the first to call a meeting when there's drama to be resolved among the players or the staff. When she has had the lead in a show and it closes after a successful run, she gets satisfaction from having led the team to that success. When not on stage, Kacee is passing her passion for making music on to others and finds it very satisfying when she sees a student in her classroom make it over some hump to become a better musician. These make the risks that come with leadership worth it for her.

Elisabeth Gortschacher – Bring the World Together to Create Better Leaders

I have yet to meet Elisabeth Gortschacher in person as I have never been to Australia and she has not visited the U.S., but we became fast friends over the phone. Born in Austria and having had a less than perfect childhood, she has been a leader since she was young, feeling it comes naturally to her.

After spending many years in nursing, Elisabeth decided to change careers and applied for a local government job she thought was a quality-management position, something not too far afield from the nursing management position she had just left. Instead she found out that it was an organizational development (OD) job, an area in which she had no experience. To her complete amazement she landed the job over forty-eight other applicants, several of whom had been in OD for many years.

The job was to develop leaders from all levels of the department, bottom to top. There was a program in place for which the organization had previously used consultants and outside vendors. The company hired Elisabeth to replace them all, putting the whole thing in her lap. One part of the program was to take people out in a sail boat and have them go overboard. Problem was, Elisabeth could not swim. Overwhelmed, she knew she had to take this on, including going overboard herself. So off she went and learned to swim, at least enough to be able to do this. "I can still remember looking into the water as I went overboard," she said, "I was terrified." She was so committed, however, to doing a great job and having everyone in the department become a great leader, that she let go of her fear and jumped in.

Elisabeth's leadership was what had the whole department complete the program successfully. Everyone had become a leader.

Adel Luzuriaga – Empowering Others in All She Does

Adel Luzuriaga embodies the definition of leadership by Lao Tse, who says that a leader,

"*...is a catalyst, and though things would not get done well if he weren't there, when they succeed he takes no credit. And because he takes no credit, credit never leaves him.*"

Five feet of ramrod-straight energy, her determination and drive are present even when she laughs. Adel is a successful real estate agent and an active voice in the community, standing up for what she believes is right even when it is inconvenient to her. The story she told me, however, is much more humble.

"My greatest success is my niece," says Adel. "She was accepted to Stanford University with a full scholarship and I know that I helped her get there. I taught her self-discipline and the importance of honoring her word, whether you feel like it or not. No stories, no excuses.

"At fifteen years old, she would be at my door five days a week between 5:30 and 6:00 am to work out with me over the whole nine weeks of her summer vacation while other kids were playing with their friends, sleeping late, whiling away their time. That's not all. After exercising with me, she then went to summer classes starting at 8:00 a.m. because she is committed to excelling in her life and career. She learned real self-discipline, such an important trait if you want to get ahead in life. It takes such strength to stay with exercise particularly in the summer when it is supposed to be time to take it a little easier. I am moved to tears," said Adel as her eyes misted over.

Sarah Manor – A Life Created through Her Commitment to Her Children

Sarah Manor was broke, her husband no longer wanted to be married, and she had no physical means of support. At that point she realized she had a decision to make: to be a victim or to step up to the plate. Sarah didn't get to think about being a leader; she had a job to do – provide for her children. She *had* to be a leader.

Having great parents who set a good example and give the right messages to their children is not a bad way to start life as a leader. Sarah had just that: her parents were successful and very supportive of her and her siblings; she had already won an award as a filmmaker by the time she had left college and was married to a successful movie producer. They lived in a lovely home in Los Angeles, had two children and went to London often to visit her parents.

Change happens to us all, and Sarah's lovely life unraveled. She had applied for a green card, her immigrant's visa to be able to live and work in the United States, but on one of her usual summer trips to London, a bureaucratic glitch caught her and she was not able to return home immediately.

This could not have happened at a worse time because before she left for London, her husband had told her that he didn't want to be married anymore. This should have been the time for them to work on their relationship, but instead she was stuck in London for six months. When she finally arrived back in Los Angeles with her children, she was a single mom, without a job or any other income.

What could she do? She wasn't sure how she would work and where to put her kids. Her commitment to her children was that they would always be in a good school. She found a pre-kindergarten program that she liked for Maya, her daughter, and as she could not afford to send Maya there, she offered to work there for free. The school's director agreed, even providing lunches for Maya and her younger brother. To keep the job, even though it was just as a volunteer, Sarah had to take a class at UCLA. Sarah took it on with gusto and completed a teaching credential in just nine months.

Sarah felt like she had been thrown in at the deep end with the job, learning as she went. The school was going through a change; there was a new head of school and a difficult transition. A new director asked Sarah where she saw herself in the future, and she said as a teacher, a strategic move for her. Sarah negotiated not only her salary, but her work schedule, standing firm on the need to leave work at the same time as her children at the end of the day; that when they were sick, she would stay home to take care of them. In return Sarah agreed to give her all. She was encouraged to get her advanced teaching credential, so once again she jumped in for another year of study.

At the end of the second year of teaching they were opening a second class like the one that Maya had gone to. Sarah was asked to be the lead teacher for that class, as she had shown her leadership skills in the classroom. She then completed her education credentials.

Just four weeks later the head of the school called her to his office. Uh-oh, she thought, this is not good, but she walked in and they were smiling. They had been really impressed with her, and a new position had opened up for her to consider: a job in administration as a curriculum coordinator.

Not sure how much respect she could expect from her co-workers after such a rapid rise, she wondered if they would feel that she had undermined them. She thought about what it would be like and wondered if she took the job in administration, would she ever get back to the classroom. Was teaching more important to her? She really needed to sit back and look at her priorities. Was she here because she wanted to be with children or merely as a means to an end? She was also told there was no guarantee they would be able to take her on next year as a kindergarten teacher, and said she would have to go back to school yet again, this time to get a master's degree. A lot of pressure.

The last week of school Sarah finally agreed to take the position.

About three months into it, she realized she liked her job, but not her title. The curriculum was there before she started and a more appropriate title would be Assistant Director. The principal agreed.

Sarah is very grateful that the school makes allowances for her children. One time, for example, Maya had a presentation to make and Sarah was able to schedule it into her workday. Whatever it is, a classroom party, anything going on in their day, Sarah is part of it; she doesn't miss anything. She has been able to build a relationship with her boss that involves a very deep level of understanding of their respective needs.

Jan Harrington – A Nice Girl with a Successful Construction Company

I have known Jan Harrington for many years, having met her while networking at Women of Pasadena, a diverse group of women active in business, corporate life, academia and community volunteering. For most of that time I knew very little about her other than she was successful in the man's world of construction.

While Jan was raising her son and daughters, the women's liberation movement of the 1960s and 1970s was creating a culture of having it all and doing it all. Jan embraced this culture and was determined to do a great job raising her children while growing a successful company and having a wonderful relationship with her husband and friends, as well as volunteering in the community. I don't know about you, but I got tired just thinking about all that.

A product of the times, she had no hesitation saying that her greatest success as a leader was being a mom of three kids and running a successful business while making sure their emotional and mental states and young minds were intact. It pleases her better than anything else. Her children are now grown and successful in their own right.

When her children were young, Jan started work when they went to school, dropping them off and picking them up at the end of the day. Once they were home, Jan and the children would sit around the table as they did their homework and she did her computer work. It was a great arrangement that meant they were there to help each other. They did it that way for years and when she shut the doors of the office at 5 to start dinner, her business was closed and anything to do with it waited until the next day. She did have a pager for emergencies, but unless that went off, business was done for the day.

The decision to grow her business slowly while her kids were growing up meant that she could stop in the middle of the day and watch their ball games and their dramatic events. She knew that many parents were not free to do that because they had a 9-5 job, and if they took a day off every month their bosses would ask them if they were serious about their job, or if they would be better off staying home with their children. Jan was happy and grateful to have the opportunity to set her own work schedule. She took on smaller, less important jobs so that she could complete them. At the beginning she did all the work herself. With careful planning she managed her day so she could be part of her children's lives. A success story for Jan and for her children.

Thinking of her children as her "clean slates," she was responsible for everything that went on them. She reaps the benefit now that they are grown, having a great relationship with them and seeing their accomplishments and how they see the world. Nothing better than being a mom. "What's the purpose of a successful business if not to share it with the ones you love?" she asked.

Ann Rector – Passionate about Children

Jan introduced me to Ann Rector, head of the Health Department for the Pasadena Unified School District. When I walked in for our appointment, there was Ann: tall, athletic-looking, a no-nonsense haircut and dressed in Dodger Blue, she was ready to take her family to a game as soon as our interview was over.

Effective as a leader in her position, it became clear very quickly that her passion is children. Prior to her current position Ann was a schoolteacher for seventeen years, working with middle school students. Although she hardly couched her words in terms of leadership, her passion came through when talking about how she enjoyed the kids. "My" kids, as she called them, "were very responsive to me ... I am a strict disciplinarian and my students knew if they stepped over the line there were consequences. While other kids were throwing books out the window, getting referrals to the principal's office, my kids were on the up and up. They respected me, I had good lesson plans, created a structured environment with known boundaries. No question that it is a very challenging age group, but they're funky, have a lot going on, but I dug it. I really liked it."

What I came away with after talking with Ann is that sometimes as leaders we can be passionate, and other times we can still be effective when we know what it takes to make a difference, to lead with others in mind rather than ourselves.

Claudette Roche – Bridging a Family Rift

Claudette Roche exudes confidence. As an actor she has learned how to present herself well, with elegant clothes and makeup that enhances her natural beauty. When she came to me as a client several years ago to help her start a business as an accent coach, I was struck by her talent. She could change accents in a sentence as easily as a pianist would play a scale on the keyboard.

Her natural abilities as a businesswoman played out quickly, and her business was a success within a very short period of time. It was not her business, however, that Claudette considers her greatest success as a leader. It was bringing her family together. Claudette's mother and her mother's half-sister had not spoken since her mother was nineteen. There was great animosity between them – a very deep rift. Claudette was determined to bring them together and eventually managed to get them in the same room, along with all her side of the family including cousins she had never met, a total of eighty people. Many had never met, and didn't even know the others existed.

"For that afternoon I got them to sit on a sofa together and talk. It was the biggest thing I ever did. No one asked me to make it happen but I saw there was a need, I placed calls and made the suggestion to have a reunion. I now have this large family that I never had before and we are all in communication with each other. So not only for me, but for some of the others, they have family that they had never had."

Kristi Toia – CEO and Empowering Leader

Kristi Toia wants to be the non-leader among leaders. This tall, poised CEO is a leader despite herself. Her stint as head of her company started when her father left on a trip and told her to run things and not to mess with anything on his desk. She didn't listen; instead she got right in there and organized things. On his return her dad turned the business over to her. She ran the company successfully, empowering staff to make decisions. Kristi brings out the best in everyone and guides the company with decisions and actions that will best benefit all – employees, vendors, customers, management and owners.

As with all the leaders I spoke with, Kristi's leadership doesn't stop with her role at her company. She is a leader all the time. Here's an example she gave me: She was driving home licking an ice cream and daydreaming when the car in front of her was hit. Kristi could have done what I have seen many people do: find the quickest way to get around the crash and be on her way home. Instead, she dropped her ice cream and went directly to help the woman who had been hit. She immediately began to organize, sending one person to call for help and another to notify the woman's next of kin, all the while sitting with the woman to calm her down and make sure she was okay until the paramedics arrived. Leadership isn't something we put on and off like a suit of clothes.

Ellen Snortland – Passion Drives Her

For the past ten plus years, Ellen Snortland, J.D., author, columnist, performer, self-defense expert and activist has been the torch bearer for me on the subject of women's rights and women's leadership. She was one of the founding board members of 50/50 Leadership and has much wisdom to share. Here are Ellen's words on leadership:

> I had a family where we were really devoted to service. They grew up in the depression. They got to see how one person can make a difference, so I had a really fertile ground for becoming a leader. However, it wasn't expected of a woman in my generation to be a leader and I had to carve that out for myself. I don't think you can be a leader without a hunger for something, mine is justice. I

most often see women and girls left out so I have my work cut out for me and as I happen to be one of those left out, I am a loud voice with big clanging ovaries.

I can credit 12-step programs with being able to let go of thinking I can control what other people think. Half will like what I do, half will not. If I can't control what other people think, then I might as well please myself. It takes that kind of unconcern for the opinion of people I don't care about anyway, which is what I need to be an opinion columnist. I also consider myself to have a rare platform to speak for people who don't have a voice – women and girls. The media is pretty much dominated by white males and the women who happen to slip through have to tip toe the patriarchal line to keep working.

Gloria Steinem completely and utterly changed my life. Gloria Steinem and this wonderful African-American woman, Florynce Kennedy came to Billings, Montana and I was one of only 20 in the audience. Despite the small numbers, they gave us 100% as if the arena was filled. She was brilliant, thought outside of the box, and really provided a vision of what it was to be a woman that went beyond gender. It was about being a global citizen. I went forward from that day to expose sexism wherever I could find it.

My mother adored Eleanor Roosevelt. I looked up to Eleanor Roosevelt and Anne Frank as a young girl, and Gloria Steinem as I grew into adulthood. I always had in the back of my mind that I would want to make Anne Frank proud of me, and then as an adult I wanted to make Gloria Steinem proud of me. They both write, are self-expressed, they tell their truth and are committed to their authentic voice.

Not long after hearing Gloria Steinem I took the est training and that was another way of looking outside the box and I thought I would devote my life to living as far out of the box as I could. I had almost died in a flood at age 19, came this close. It was a profound experience and from then on I didn't care anymore, life is not a rehearsal, I could be gone tomorrow.

I took an event which could have squelched me: confronting a burglar who almost knifed me, and made it a transformative event. I turned it into a life mission. Rather than letting him stab me I screamed so loudly that he dropped the knife and ran away and that led me into a deep investigation of why no-one had told me what to do if someone was violent around me. I thought that was so weird. So I became an expert at why women have the kind of relationship they do with violence when we are surrounded by it. Why is it that so many women are clueless, including me? I was ignorant.

There were no manuals about why women and girls were raised to be physically helpless so I stepped into that gap. I really didn't want to write a book but I knew I had to. This book had to be written and I know that I have saved lives with it. I get emails from people saying, "Thank you, this completely changed my life. I read your book and I was able to stop a rape that could have turned into a murder." That is satisfying, it keeps me going against great odds. People are not hungry to know they should find out about how to defend themselves until something bad happens. I am trying to shift that into prevention instead of remedy. I am, and will continue to be, like one of those dogs that keep barking and barking and barking.

Doing what needs to be done, stepping into the gap, this is what Ellen and several of these leaders have done. There is no *them* out there – as in leave it up to them to fix it. Sometimes we are it. There's no one else willing to take the risk and provide whatever is missing.

Pamela Kightlinger – Doing what needs to be done
Pamela Kightlinger, who was not sure she fit the bill of being a leader, is an example of someone who doesn't need a title. She always looks for ways to reach a solution that will serve the good of many, never just herself.

She grew up in a family of regular people around families who were mostly poor. She went to college but didn't graduate. She considers herself a leader only in that she has information to share.

She had to learn to be assertive. Growing up she didn't speak up, but she reached a point where she knew she needed to. It took practice. She was all over women's equality, but personally was only giving it lip-service, occasionally speaking forcefully about it, but looking back her actions didn't reflect it.

Here's a story Pamela heard of a young guy who is asking an old-timer how he stays off drugs. The old-timer says, "I don't do drugs and I don't argue." The young guy scratches his head and says that there has to be more to it than that, to which the old-timer answers, "You may be right."

Pamela's best friend has been a great role model for her, even though she is of a similar age. Pamela's friend came to California when she was twenty and went to work as a secretary for a small refrigeration company. She's one of those people who just does things, takes things on. This is what she did at this company until she was practically running it. She worked there for a few years then had the opportunity to buy the company, becoming the only woman licensed refrigeration contractor in the United States. She even created a device that is now in lots of hotels around the country. She sees a need and just goes on and does it.

Pamela was an immigration paralegal, a branch of the law that relies on that skill, and realized that what she was doing was valuable and that she was doing it well, with authority and autonomy.

"I must admit I like being a leader," Pamela told me. "I especially like looking at the big picture, the possibilities, how it can work, how it can best be done. I like the details too, once I get involved with it.

"Kindness, even-handedness, fairness are key; those encompass everything. It takes a certain degree of strength and risk-taking and intelligence, but kindness and fairness have to bring all that together to make it worthwhile." This is how Pamela sums up her take on leadership.

Sharon Roszia – Adoption Specialist

I was introduced to Sharon Roszia many years ago by a mutual friend who thought we should meet. Despite the enormous impact she has as a leader in the world of adoption, she is always looking to learn and consider how she can pass on her wisdom to others. Here is what she has to say:

> I was a leader in junior high, president of the Girls Cabinet. What I realized then is that I am most comfortable when I am in a leadership role. I am not that comfortable being a follower. That has sometimes gotten me in trouble with my superiors!

Two things happened in junior high, I took a leadership position and I took a speech class. I found I was perfectly comfortable standing up and talking to just about anyone or any group. In my family I was put down for that. My father nicknamed me the "Top Sargent" [*sic*] and it was meant as a put-down. He would have framed it as being bossy, and I probably was being bossy. I had to mature and learn to listen, and lead, not boss!

I moved into the world of adoption after graduate school. I started raising a lot of questions about policy and practice in the field, challenging the system and creating new perspectives; speaking out at national conferences; writing books and eventually speaking around the world.

When I think about leadership I think about role modeling, innovation, and bringing the best out in other people. My work has led me to taking on a mentorship role to equip others who want to lead. I do that by being available to them and not hesitating to point out both strengths and areas that need improvement. I love to support their creativity.

Self-awareness, constant growth and learning, risk taking, creativity, a willingness to stand out: these are all elements of what it takes to lead. A leader knows when to step up and be visible and when to step back and let things unfold with quiet guidance. It has been one of the hardest things for me to learn. I used to think I had to be out front — like a drum major. What a really bright staff member taught me was that it was necessary for me to be quiet and let my role modeling and things I had taught take root and let others take credit for what they were doing. So for me empowerment is a large piece of leadership.

I think big egos can get in the way of good leadership. Good leaders know when to let go; when to push their chicks out of the nest. Leadership through power, ego and fear is destructive.

Philosophically I have been moving more and more away from duality thinking into oneness. There is a Hopi saying that things will change when we move from two hearts to one heart recognizing that everyone's heartbeat is the same. When we embrace this truth, leadership can take on another dimension. We say "Namaste – may the spirit in me recognize the spirit in you." We are all one, that what happens to one happens to all of us. We are not isolated and leaders have a responsibility because what they say and do ripples outwards, it just keeps going – inter-generationally, across states and boundaries of every sort.

One of my leadership role models was a wordsmith. She honed her use of words to really say what she meant. If I made a statement, she would often challenge me, "do you really mean that?" I might say I understood something or someone and she would challenge me saying that she didn't think I did understand. The word "understand" means that you would be willing to stand under those words and have them fall on your head. She had me start looking at language in a whole different way. Language has always flowed through me easily; I have never had to search for words. She really taught me to stop and make sure that what was coming out of my mouth was exactly what I meant.

I am sometimes asked what has kept me working in this field for over five decades. It is an evolving field which keeps it very interesting. The need to keep learning makes it exciting. No two adoptions are the same and each brings its unique challenges. A good leader will never know enough. Maybe it's God's way of keeping egos in check.

I think there are highly educated leaders with many degrees like professors. There are visionary leaders who cogitate and dream. I would never classify myself as an erudite, professorial, research-based leader. I would say I am a visionary leader, not an intellectual leader. A lot of leaders in the world who are the visionaries are shifting consciousness in their field of work.

I rarely create in isolation, I love a team. What leaders do is recognize their strengths and their deficits and find people to partner with who are leaders in those areas where they are weaker. I have come to the conclusion that I am a leader because I partnered with really great people.

As a leader, I have doubts every day. Visionary leaders have to realize they have to make sacrifices; they may be ridiculed for their ideas and the chances they take in their fields. They may have had to give up a lot to achieve what they wanted to accomplish. One of the things that visionary leadership has is the reputation for being odd, unprofessional, "woo-woo," too California or West Coast, and yet I truly believe that all the really rich ideas that will change the planet come from such leaders. They are the iconoclasts and not shrinking violets. They are pulled to make changes so people can be treated more humanely. They ask a lot of questions and have to learn to ask the right questions.

Sometimes leadership comes through learning, making mistakes, and taking risks. Sharon is a great example of a path that is rich, satisfying and has an impact on many people.

Dr. Shelby Dietrich – Physician Bringing Health Care to All

Dr. Shelby Dietrich, mother of Ann Rector and a retired physician, was involved with an organization in its infancy, *Young and Healthy*. This group's mission is to bring health care to uninsured and underinsured children, linking doctors and medical advisors with the children. The referral base is mostly the public schools. School nurses see children who need care and who can't find it. Dr. Dietrich became the president and pushed the organization forward. In the 1990s, it was her major activity. She was making a difference and speaking as if such leadership were an everyday occurrence, which of course it is not. Here's what Shelby had to say about leadership:

> I was a leader in my specific field internationally, a specialist in the care of hemophiliacs. At Orthopedic Hospital in Los Angeles, we had the largest center in the country next to New York during the 1970s and 1980s and I was director of that center. I was very active in the World Federation of Hemophilia, leading other countries, other doctors, trying to improve the standards and improve the care worldwide.
>
> My life was very stressed during the time of the AIDS epidemic. Treating patients; trying to do the right thing; trying to explain it. I was the leader and

setting the standards. To this day I am not sure if I did the right thing. Leadership carries a very heavy responsibility when dealing with life and death standards. I just had to concentrate on what they were receiving. At that time nationally about 10,000 were infected, locally several hundred. AIDS victims fell like flies. That's when my leadership was tried to the max. I had to keep morale up in the staff and I am not sure if I did a good job. I took care of the patients, they were very grateful we didn't desert them. I have a heavy sense of responsibility. There were infectious disease cases to treat, hospital administrators to pacify; it was a terrible time.

My mother and grandmother were both role models. My grandmother was the first President of the Democratic Women's Club and President of the local women's club in the 30's. She saw things she wanted to do. My mother was not very comfortable with the leadership role, but took it on anyway. Family is the most important model.

I remember an incident in my youth, I was in college. I was home from university at some holiday and I was getting together with some girlfriends. We were debating where to go for lunch and I finally said let's go to the xyz restaurant. Then one of the others piped up, saying that she had just mentioned that same restaurant but nobody listened to her, so why are you listening to Shelby? That left me wondering why.

I will answer Dr. Dietrich's question. It was because she was a leader and her friends knew it, so when Shelby spoke, they listened.

8

SOME FINAL THOUGHTS

As well as the leadership characteristics already discussed, passion, audaciousness and creative thinking jumped out at me from meeting with these leaders.

With all of the people I interviewed, their passion was evident. Ellen burns with a drive to make women's safety a priority in life; Kacee lives for singing and performing; Leigh delights in bringing art to children; Jan, Ria and Sarah have a strong commitment to their children, which has shaped what their own lives are about. The power of their feelings comes through. Think about the times you have listened to someone in a leadership position and have been left wondering if they really have an interest in what they are doing or talking about, or if they are just "doing their job." The results are always telling. Steve Jobs was passionate about designing and bringing innovative technology to the world. When he left Apple, the company went downhill because that passion did not burn for the mercenary who took control. When Steve Jobs returned, Apple came alive again, and it has thrived.

Just going along with things is the opposite of leadership, and sometimes it takes sheer audacity to stand up and express your opinion or take a risk. Ria had audacity when she came across a man at the airport who was verbally abusing his wife and son, and asked him to stop demeaning them.

I remember once being on a temporary job assignment, and the person I worked for asked me about a leaf on the painting by his desk. I looked at the painting, which had no leaves in it, and wondered what on earth he was talking about. I told him that I could not see the leaf. He smiled as he pointed to the frame where he had put a leaf that a student had given him. I was looking at the picture in the frame and was blind to everything around it. My mind was made up, closed to everything but the picture itself. In that moment I learned the meaning of the expression "outside the box." I had taken everything so literally that when asked, I could not even see something inches away, and I wondered what else in life I was missing. How was my creativity locked up, and how could I break free?

Having learned a lot along the way, including the fact that suffering is optional, I think about giraffes when I have a hard time seeing the bright side and it seems as if my compass is stuck on *tough*. With their long necks, giraffes can pick up their heads and see farther away. I realized that if I could also pick my head up and out of the day-to-day, I could get to *easy* instead of *tough*. Then I could readjust my attitude and see a more positive horizon.

In place of suffering, what I found was choice. This was a hard concept to take in at first, but I came to realize I really do have a choice in everything. I might not like the consequences of certain choices — say, if I quit work and have no way to support myself, I would be homeless — not a choice I want to make. But realizing that I can choose my attitude gives me a lot of freedom. Viktor

Frankl, a psychiatrist who had been imprisoned in a concentration camp during World War II, realized that,

> *"Everything can be taken from a man but one thing: the last of the human freedoms—to choose one's attitude in any given set of circumstances, to choose one's own way."*

When I read his book, *Man's Search for Meaning*, from which this quote was taken, I realized that my problems are petty in the overall scheme of things. So rather than feeling like I had earned the right to feel sorry for myself given the story of my life so far, I realized I could change my thinking and my actions and see my life change. I could create a new beginning.

Whether from these leaders or from those who are better known, it is clear that being a leader is about stepping up rather than hoping someone else will.

I hope you take away from these stories the knowledge that there is no one recipe for becoming a leader. And as for *rules* of leadership, it seems there are as many styles and types of leaders and leadership as there are books written on the subject. What separates the most effective and enduring leaders from the mercenaries is the commitment to make a difference for more than oneself. Leadership is not about titles, education, or money; it is about integrity, action and caring.

I would love to hear about your leadership and what you have taken on. You can write to me at Pauline@PaulineField.com.

ABOUT THE AUTHOR

 As a kid, Pauline Field would avoid reading and writing at all costs. Not until college did she start to enjoy both. Now she has several other books waiting to be written.

She became impassioned about leadership in 2005 when she discovered how few women were actually in leadership positions in any and every walk of life, so she founded 50/50 Leadership, a nonprofit promoting women's equal leadership.

Currently working as a Research Analyst, she is the former COO (not CEO) of a global management consulting agency and management consultant for almost thirty years.

Pauline has been active in the community and although she has received many awards, she is most proud of being the mother of Adrian and also a grandmother. She lives with her partner and soulmate Barry in Pasadena, California.

Pauline would love to hear from you. You can email her directly at Pauline@PaulineField.com.

Fifty percent of the profits from the sale of the book will be donated to 50/50 Leadership, a nonprofit organization promoting women's equal leadership.